HENRI STIERLIN

PHOTOS: ANNE AND HENRI STIERLIN

TURKEY

FROM THE SELÇUKS
TO THE OTTOMANS

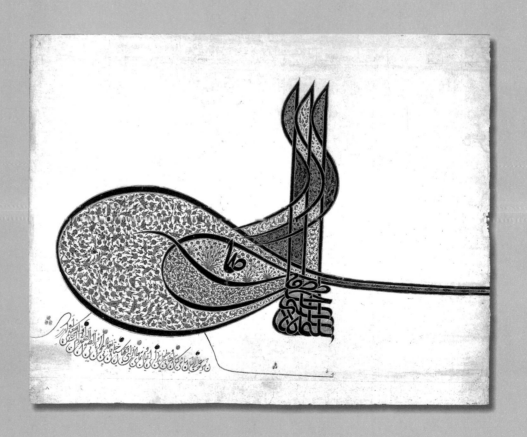

TASCHEN

KÖLN LISBOA LONDON NEW YORK PARIS TOKYO

Page 3
Signature of a decree (*firman*)
by Sultan Süleyman, dated
1555–1560. This official document
presents ornamental lettering of
extreme refinement, akin to the
exquisite floral tiling that covers
the monuments of the period.
(The Metropolitan Museum of Art,
New York, Rogers Fund, 1938,
38.149.1)

Page 5
In his palace, the Topkapı Sarayı,
with its polychrome tile revetment, Sultan Süleyman the
Magnificent sits enthroned
beneath a domed ceiling. Before
him is a courtyard with murmuring
fountain. Following the Persian
tradition, the Turkish miniaturists
of the Tabriz school represented
architecture in tiered perspective.
From the *Sulaymannama* (*Book of
Süleyman*), completed in 1558.
(Library of the Topkapı Sarayı
Museum, Istanbul)

© 1998 Benedikt Taschen Verlag GmbH
Hohenzollernring 53, D-50672 Köln

Editor-in-chief: Angelika Taschen, Cologne
Edited by Susanne Klinkhamels, Caroline Keller, Cologne
Co-edited by Karl Georg Cadenbach, Düren
Design and layout: Marion Hauff, Milan
English translation: Chris Miller, Oxford

Printed in Italy
ISBN 3-8228-7767-0

Contents

INTRODUCTION

Turkish Expansion in the Middle East

Islamic architecture has flourished in Turkey as in few other regions of the Mediterranean. During the reigns of the Selçuk and Ottoman sultans, schools (*madrasas*), mosques (*camis*), bathhouses (*hammams*), caravanserais (*khans* or *hans*), tombs (*türbes*) and palaces were built throughout Asia Minor and subsequently in European Turkey and Istanbul. Among them were many masterpieces. The flowering of Turkish architecture between the thirteenth and nineteenth centuries represents one of the high points of Islamic art.

The Turks followed in the footsteps of the Roman, Greek and Byzantine civilisations. They arrived in Anatolia from the seventh century A. D., the last of a floodtide of invasions from Central Asia that swept before it the established order of the ancient world.

The Origins of the Turks

It is generally thought that the nomadic Turkish tribes originated in the forests of the Altai Mountains, where the borders of Siberia, Mongolia and China meet. They were related to the Huns, the Mongols, the Uighurs and the Oghuz and to other Turkic peoples now known under Chinese names: Xiongnu, Shatuo and others. By their migrations through the vast plains of Central Asia they forged an important link between the Pacific and Western Europe.

Whole tribes of this ethnic group were frequently on the march. They made incursions into disintegrating empires. They overran the Great Wall of China; they penetrated the Roman *limes* (frontier) along the Rhine and the Danube. When conquest was not the motive, famine resulting from drought or climatic change sometimes forced them to plunder the granaries and provender of sedentary peoples.

By 552, the Turkic tribes had become the masters of a vast empire of the steppes. Their military prowess brought major conquests, in particular that of Transoxiana, where they came into contact with the Sassanid Persians. They controlled the approaches to the Aral and Caspian Seas. Some tribes were in conflict with Byzantium, others with the wave of Arab expansion that had resulted in the defeat of the Chinese armies at Talas in 751.

The finest Turkish troops at this point enlisted as soldier-slave *mamluks* in the service of the Samanids of Iran and the Abbasids of Baghdad. They converted *en masse* to Sunni Islam and entered into fruitful contact with the developing Arab civilisation, which, in the eighth to ninth centuries, created a flourishing empire stretching from Northern Africa to the gates of India.

In 962, a *mamluk* in the service of the Samanids seized power and established the kingdom of the Ghaznevids on the river Iaxartes (modern Syr-Dar'ya). Tügrül Beg (1038–1063) overran it and took power, founding the Selçuk Sultanate. Having first captured the capital, Ghazni, he conquered Persia and moved his capital to Isfahan in 1051. There he formed an alliance with the Caliphate in the struggle against the Shiites. Naming himself "Protector of the Caliphate", he installed a garrison at

Baghdad in 1055. The last representatives of the Abbasid dynasty thus found themselves in thrall to their "praetorian guard".

Alp Arslan succeeded Tügrül Beg as sultan (1063–1073); under his rule, Aleppo was captured, Armenia conquered, and a decisive victory against the Byzantines under the emperor Roman IV Diogenes was won in 1071 at Manzikert in the Anatolian plateau. This battle ended resistance to Turkish domination of Asia Minor. Thereafter the invading tribes occupied the whole country, spreading out to the Mediterranean, the Aegean, the Sea of Marmara and the Black Sea. For Alp Arslan, this huge land bordered on three sides by the sea was a kind of *finis terrae*, the end of the earth. Here, where successive waves of conquest had established some of the great civilisations of the ancient world – the Hittites, the Persians led by Darius and Xerxes, the Greeks by Alexander, the Romans by Pompey and Trajan, the Byzantines by Heraclius, the Sassanids by Khosru, the Omayyads by Mu'awiya and many others – the Turks settled and made their home.

This branch of the Turkish "nation" formed the Rum Selçuk Empire (1073–1308). The term Rum, derived from *Rumi* (Romans), distinguished them from the Turks established in Persia (the Great Selçuks); it also indicated that the authority of Constantinople was now subsumed by that of the Turks. In the fifteenth century this authority expanded still further when one of the most dynamic of the Turkish tribes, the Osmanlı or Ottomans, founded medieval and modern Turkey, whose empire extended throughout the Near East and into Eastern Europe and Northern Africa, from Egypt to the Atlantic.

While the Rum Selçuk troops were occupying the shores of Anatolia, other Turkish armies were extending their conquests. Under Melik Şah (1073–1092) they took Transoxiana, the Kirman and Syria, and captured the cities of Damascus and Jerusalem. The capture of the Holy City caused great alarm throughout Europe; the Selçuk invasion was seen as undermining the balance of power between the Arabs and the European kingdoms. Concerned at the threat to Christian pilgrims in Palestine and afraid that access to the Holy Land would be cut off, the Western nations exhorted their peoples to embark on a Crusade. In 1095, Pope Urban II solemnly declared that Jerusalem must be liberated, and with it Golgotha, the site of Christ's Passion. War was therefore declared between the Christian armies and the forces of the Selçuks and Arabs, and ended only with the Christian capture of Jerusalem. Meanwhile the war extended to Anatolia, where the much weakened *basileus* (ruler) of Constantinople, the Crusader lords and the Armenians confronted not only the Selçuks but fresh waves of invading Mongols, who included many Turkish warriors in their ranks. These invasions by Mongol hordes continued intermittently for another 150 years. In the mid-thirteenth century, the Mongols advanced as far as Konya but then retreated, to the great relief of the Selçuks, who could thus pursue unhindered their assimilation of the former Byzantine domains.

The Foundations of the Turkish "Nation"

The community of the Turkish tribes was founded on their language. The Ural-Altaic linguistic family to which it belongs includes Mongol, Finnish, Hungarian, and perhaps Korean and Ainu (northern Japan). It is an agglutinative language, functioning through the use of suffixes, and comprises just one declension and a single conjugation.

The earliest written Turkish characters derived from Sogdian (a combination of runiform and Uighur characters), but after their conversion to Islam the Turks turned to the Arabic alphabet even though it is unsuited to their language. This practice continued until 1928, when, under the sway of Mustafa Kemal (later Atatürk), they adopted the Roman alphabet. For the great majority of modern Turks, this decision irremediably divided them from their past. The numerous

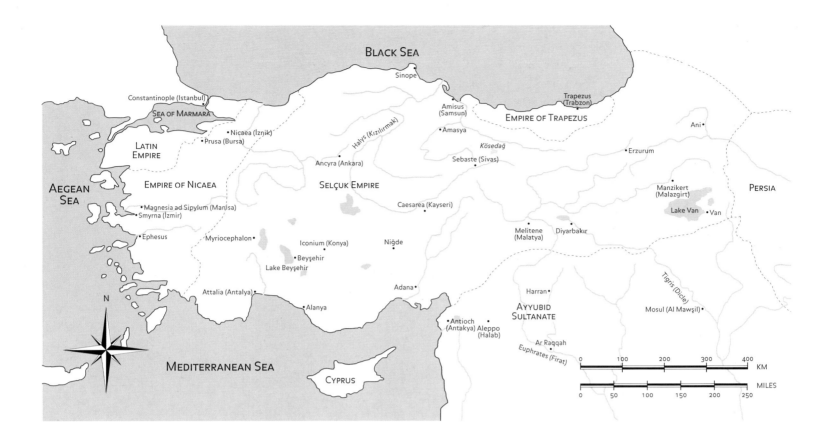

The map shows the following labels:

BLACK SEA

Sinope
Constantinople (Istanbul)
SEA OF MARMARA
Amisus (Samsun)
Trapezus (Trabzon)
EMPIRE OF TRAPEZUS
Ani
LATIN EMPIRE
Nicaea (Iznik)
Prusa (Bursa)
Amasya
Kösedağ
Erzurum
Sebaste (Sivas)
Ancyra (Ankara)
AEGEAN SEA
EMPIRE OF NICAEA
SELÇUK EMPIRE
Manzikert (Malazgirt)
PERSIA
Magnesia ad Sipylum (Manisa)
Smyrna (Izmir)
Caesarea (Kayseri)
Lake Van
Van
Ephesus
Myriocephalon
Iconium (Konya)
Niğde
Melitene (Malatya)
Diyarbakır
Beyşehir
Lake Beyşehir
Halys (Kızılırmak)
Tigris (Dicle)
Attalia (Antalya)
Adana
Harran
AYYUBID SULTANATE
Mosul (Al Mawşil)
N
Alanya
Antioch (Antakya) Aleppo (Halab)
Ar Raqqah
Euphrates (Firat)
MEDITERRANEAN SEA
CYPRUS

0 100 200 300 400 KM
0 50 100 150 200 250 MILES

The Rum Selçuk sultanate

The Anatolian Empire of the Rum Selçuks in the thirteenth century. In western Anatolia, only the Empire of Nicaea, and the Latin Empire created in the aftermath of the Crusaders' capture of Constantinople in 1204, stand out against the Turks. In the north, the Byzantines still retain the Empire of Trebizond (the ancient Trapezus). In the south-east, the Rum Sultanate borders on the Ayyubid Sultanate and the Persian Empire.

untransliterated texts from the past are accessible only to the erudite, and require scholarly work before they can again form part of the national heritage.

Turks and Persians are exceptional in that when they converted to Islam they did not adopt the Arabic language of the Koran. Arabic became the language of Egypt and North Africa, of Palestine, Syria and Mesopotamia. Unlike those countries that saw in Arabic the bond of a common culture, the Turkish sultans remained loyal to their native language.

The culture that the Turks brought with them to Anatolia was that of nomadic or semi-nomadic tribes, skilful warriors dependent on a pastoral economy. They lived in felt tents called *yurts*, and their furniture was sparse and light, consisting mainly of carpets, hangings, cushions, and so on. Shamans – priestly magi who were in touch with the divine and practised divination – were the custodians of traditional knowledge.

In their nomadic state, the Turks had scarcely felt the influence of the sedentary peoples they displaced, whom they encountered only during raids and battles. Before they settled in a land of ancient civilisation, they had only the most rudimentary notions of architecture and art.

Over the course of their long migrations of the first millennium, the Turks had come into contact with China: first the Han dynasty, then the Six Dynasties (221–589) and finally the Sui dynasty (561–618). Though not as violent as their clashes with the later Tang and Sung dynasties – the Imperial throne was at times occupied by Turco-Mongols until the fourteenth century – these confrontations took place over a vast timespan, and Chinese influence is easily discernible in the culture of the fifteenth-century Timurids.

Further west, the Turkish conquests of the ninth and tenth centuries in Transoxania and Khorasan (Persia) – and subsequently throughout the Middle East – placed the Selçuks at the centre of a region of widely varying cultural tendencies and traditions. They were in close contact with the Persians, the Arabs, the Syrians, the Armenians and the Byzantines. They drew upon these cultures to create a vast pool of knowledge.

A portico in the Çifte Minare
Medresesi at Erzurum
In the mid-thirteenth century,
Turkish architecture entered
a new and rigorous phase
expressed in four-centred arches
strengthened by tie-beams, and
columns whose rhythms are
emphasised by geometric
ornamentation.

Their reign in Bukhara, Samarkand and Isfahan was consequently marked by an unprecedented flowering of the architectural arts. New techniques of roofing and decoration were discovered, such as pointed vaults, domes mounted on squinches, and *iwans* with stalactite work. And the decorative arts – architectural stoneware, ceramics, calligraphy, books and miniatures – also made prodigious strides.

The Persian Selçuk sultans not only promoted the construction of mosques and Koranic schools but were munificent patrons of the arts in general. Their patronage attracted poets, painters, scholars, astronomers and physicians. On occasion, sultans simply summoned to the court the artistic and cultural élite of the country and put it to work for the greater glory of the government. China's influence was to be reckoned with amongst the Selçuk potters, as the wonderful Nishapur ware testifies.

The cultural appetite shown by the Persian Selçuk courts resulted from the assimilation by its rulers, no longer nomads, of the intellectual currents of the Arabo-Persian world. The sultans – and their courtiers, who exercised considerable influence – took advantage of the intellectual resources offered by the countries over which they had absolute power.

None of this was yet true of the other Selçuk tribes, who continued their conquest of Anatolia. It took a long period of acculturation before these tribes showed any aptitude for urban life, and longer still before they began to appreciate the decorative arts and create a style of their own. It is said that, at the time of the Third Crusade (1189–1192), the Selçuk sultans still spent the summer in tents outside the city walls of their capital, Konya.

By 1071, the Turkish invasion of Anatolia was in full swing. A century and a half went by before the architectural and artistic flowering of the Selçuks of Anatolia was under way. Their first concerns were military; they had to repulse the attacks not only of Christian forces in the form of the Crusaders and Byzantines, but also of the troops of the Islamic Ayyubid dynasty. They also had to defend their territory against the ambitions of rival Turkish clans, such as the Danishmendites.

The unification of Anatolia was the work of Kılıç Arslan II (1155–1192). After defeating the Byzantines in the Battle of Myriocephalon in 1176, he turned his attention to the Danishmendites and routed them. The Crusaders besieged Konya in 1190, but Keyhüsrev I (1192–1210) subsequently restored the entire territory to Selçuk hands.

It is something of a paradox that the Selçuks should at first have ignored the Byzantine artistic and architectural heritage. The architectural skills of these former nomads were learnt primarily from Northern Syria and from Armenia. The Syrians were great masters of stone-carving, building innumerable churches and monasteries in what became, after the Arab reconquest, the "dead" Christian towns north of Aleppo.

The Armenians were wonderful architects and stone-cutters. But their destiny was a tragic one. Their new capital, Ani, was pillaged by the Byzantines before falling into the hands of the Selçuks. They then attempted to establish a refuge in South Anatolia. In 1080, a Bagratid prince founded the kingdom of Little Armenia in the mountains of Cilicia. These refugees allied themselves with the Crusaders of the Latin Empire but took care to remain friendly with the Selçuk sultans.

Teams of artisans and builders from two communities all but swamped by the Islamic tide thus placed themselves at the service of the Anatolian Selçuk sultans. Over the next century, they, and the labour force they recruited *in situ*, built for their new masters an imposing series of monuments, which date from the early thirteenth to the first decades of the fourteenth century.

The Rum Selçuks and their Public Works

Two main objectives seem to have propelled the Anatolian sultans in the vast programme of public building that they initiated. The first of these was to ensure the diffusion of the purest Sunnite orthodoxy, a goal that they pursued by constructing a great number of *madrasas* or Koranic schools. The second was to provide safe means of communication over the length and breadth of their territory, in order to promote international trade. This they did by constructing a chain of fortified caravanserais (*khans* or *hans*) studding the roads that linked Anatolia, the Mediterranean and the Black Sea; they were built one day's travel – around 30 km – apart, and covered the north-south and east-west axes of the Selçuk domain.

At key points in this network of caravan routes linking the ports of Samsun (ancient Amisus), Antalya (Attalia) and Silifke (Seleucia) stood the ancient cities whose names had changed with their rulers: Konya (Iconium), Kayseri (Caesarea) and Sivas (Sebaste). The routes meant that the Anatolian plateau could be crossed without having to pass through the perilous Straits Settlements or the Aegean, both of which were in Byzantine hands.

The Selçuk public works comprised mosques, which answered the need for daily prayer in the cities, and baths or *hammams*, which followed ancient tradition in bringing the luxury of water to the arid steppes. But the *madrasas* also provided an ideological component and the caravanserais an economic one. This policy showed

Conflict with central Europe
The reign of Süleyman the Magnificent was one of conquests. In 1529, the Sultan's janissaries besieged Vienna, the capital of the Emperor Charles V. The failure of the siege put an end to Ottoman expansion in Europe. Miniature from the *Sulaymannama* or *Book of Süleyman* of 1558, showing Belgrade under attack; it fell in 1521. (Library of the Topkapı Sarayı Museum, Istanbul)

**Staging-posts for the
Anatolian caravans**
On the high plateaux of Asia
Minor, the caravanserais built in
the thirteenth century by the Rum
Selçuks exhibit superlative
vaulted spaces resembling the
naves of medieval churches. The
winter hall of the Sultanhanı near
Kayseri, dating from 1232, was
built to accommodate merchants
travelling to or from Central Asia
or the Mediterranean.

admirable foresight. The Selçuk territory soon became both a centre of religious enlightenment, which found expression in the works of mystics such as Hacı Bektaş (Arabic: Hajji Bektash) and Mevlana (Jala al-Din Rumi), and a major trading centre that profited from its position at the meeting-point of East and West.

The caravans that arrived from northern Persia carried precious goods to the southern shores of the Black Sea (silk, carpets, and Kipchak slaves). There the goods were transferred to other caravans, which took them over the high plateaux to the Mediterranean. From there, commercial fleets distributed them to Ayyubid Syria and the Mamluk kingdom of Cairo. And goods also went to the West, thanks to the Genoan and Venetian trading posts that underpinned a commerce facilitated by the presence of the Crusaders.

Page 13
An ornamented façade
The façade of the İnce Minare
Medresesi at Konya, built in 1265,
displays sumptuous carved
ornamentation, typical of the
Selçuk art of Anatolia. Bands of
inscription alternate with geometrical and floral motifs.

The centre of Anatolian mysticism
In Konya stands the mausoleum of Mevlana or Jala al-Din Rumi, the mystic and poet, born in Balkh, who died in Konya in 1273. It is the centre for the monks called whirling dervishes, who attain spiritual illumination through the trance induced by their constantly turning dance. Mevlana's *türbe* (mausoleum) with its revetment of green tiles (green is the colour of Islam) is the goal of many pilgrims.

The Selçuk reign thus brought a period of exceptional prosperity; the abundance of traded goods and the new vitality imparted to Sunnite Islam by the *madrasas* combined to produce a fine harvest of civil and religious buildings, the construction of major road networks with bridges and caravanserais for merchants and travellers, and considerable urban development.

The Apogee of the Ottoman Empire

This policy of public works – expanded to meet the scale of the huge Ottoman empire – continued under the sultans of Istanbul. By then Turkish power had given rise to one of the greatest empires in history, one that, at the time of the Renaissance, connected the Mediterranean basin with the Near East.

The rise of the tribe of Osman was to bring the Turkish nation to the apogee of its power. The tribe moved from Khorasan to settle in western Anatolia in the thirteenth century, establishing itself south of Nicaea to join forces with the Selçuk campaigns against Byzantium. The policy of attrition conducted by the Sultans of İznik (ancient Nicaea), Bursa (Prusa) and Edirne (Adrianople) gnawed at the perimeter of the Byzantine holdings until these were reduced to the city of Constantinople within its land and sea walls, and a few possessions on the shores of the Black Sea, such as Trabzon (Trebizond/Trapezus).

Constantinople had already suffered during its capture by the Crusaders in 1204. Now the Sultans ordered siege after siege. In 1453, a final assault carried the town. The forces of Mehmet II Fatih (the Conqueror) entered a largely depopulated city. With the exception of Haghia Sophia and certain other churches (soon transformed into mosques), the town was delivered over to the pillaging troops. Constantinople would henceforth be Istanbul.

The *külliye* at Edirne
From 1365 until the capture of Constantinople in 1453, Edirne was the Ottoman capital. Bayezit II (1481–1512), who was attached to the former capital, caused the architect Hayrettin to build a religious complex or *külliye* in the city; the complex marks an important event in the evolution of Ottoman architecture. It comprises a mosque, a *madrasa* and hospitals, all dating from 1484–1488.

The Ottoman capital moved from İznik to Bursa, and thence to Edirne. With each successive transfer came progress in the art of architecture. Under the influence of Byzantine buildings, the Ottomans originated a style of their own, which found its full expression in the reign of Bayezit II (1481–1512). The monuments built by the architect Hayrettin at Edirne and Istanbul exhibit a classicism that anticipated the masterworks of the mid-sixteenth century.

Thereafter Ottoman hegemony extended steadily into Europe and the Near East, particularly under Selim I (1512–1520) and especially in the brilliant reign of Süleyman II the Magnificent (1520–1566), which transformed the Osmanlı empire into an international power to be reckoned with. Charles V of France was forced to contend with this new power, and François I sought an alliance with it. Süleyman was the patron of the great architect Sinan, of whose many admirable mosques the best known is perhaps the Süleymaniye. Some of the most recognisable landmarks of present-day Istanbul date from this period.

The dome of the Süleymaniye
Sinan's Süleymaniye was inaugurated in 1550; it marks a high point in his career and in Ottoman architecture. Analogies with Haghia Sophia invested the Süleymaniye with a symbolic significance intended to reinforce Sultan Süleyman's connections with the Emperor Justinian, in whose reign the Byzantine basilica was built. The central dome buttressed by semi-domes and tympana constituted an unmistakable reference to the basilica and thus to the continuity of Süleyman's imperial inheritance.

Under Selim II, Sinan built what is widely regarded as his masterpiece, and one of the greatest achievements of Ottoman architecture: the Selimiye at Edirne. In the architects that followed in Sinan's footsteps, no comparable inspiration or audacity can be found. By the time Da'ud Aĝa was building the Yeni Valide Camii and Mehmet Aĝa the Blue Mosque of Ahmet I, stagnation had set in, and the imagination, coherence and audacity of Sinan were reduced to traditional formulas.

The Ottoman Empire nevertheless had some surprises in store, and in the eighteenth and nineteenth centuries a kind of Turkish "rococo" originated, exemplified in the Nusretiye Camii, in which Western influence is manifest.

Over six centuries, the course of Turkish architecture led from the Selçuk epoch and the early Ottoman style of İznik and Bursa to the classicism of Edirne, attaining its apotheosis in the masterpieces of Sinan. The quest for elegant spatial solutions was the central thread in this development, and makes the Turkish architectural tradition one of the most original and powerful in the history of world architecture.

The Selimiye in Edirne
In 1574, during the reign of Süleyman's successor, Selim II, Sinan completed his greatest masterpiece: the Selimiye in Edirne. The central space of this sultanic mosque is octagonal; tympana alternate with squinches. The internal space, flooded with light, lies beneath a dome 31.5 m in diameter and 45 m above the floor.

ANATOLIA UNDER THE SELÇUKS

The Monuments of the Turkish Sultans During the Thirteenth and Fourteenth Centuries

When the Selçuk tribes invaded Anatolia after the Battle of Manzikert in 1071, they took over a region long contested by Christians and Muslims. Control had alternated between Arab and Byzantine hands for centuries. Islam had been a major force in eastern Asia Minor since 663. The rulers of Isauria made inroads into the Islamic lands; Constantine V captured Melitene (modern Malatya) in 751. During the reign of Nicephorus I an Arab raid reached Ancyra (Ankara). In 878, under the Macedonian Dynasty, Basil I returned Cappadocia and the Taurus to Byzantine control. In 962, Nicephorus Phocas regained Cilicia and Aleppo, and added Northern Syria to his domains; it was quickly retaken, but reconquered by Basil II (994–999).

Even before Manzikert, the eleventh century had seen the advent of the Turks in eastern Asia Minor. The Selçuks had burnt Melitene in 1057, and had sacked Sebaste (now Sivas) in 1059 and Caesarea (Kayseri) in 1067. In 1074, they overcame the Byzantine armies in Cappadocia and settled there. Turkish territory in western Asia Minor continued to expand. In 1081, the Sultan Süleyman established the Rum Selçuk capital at Nicaea (İznik).

The Turks settled permanently in Anatolia, and since then it has been Turkish. Neither the Crusaders nor the rulers of the Latin Empire – not even the passage of the Mongol Golden Horde (1243) – wrested Anatolia from the Turkish grip, though small pockets of Byzantine resistance, such as Trebizond (Trabzon), remained.

The Arabic and Persian Heritage

The traces of Arab occupation in eastern Anatolia were few and far apart. They consisted mainly of mosques, whose classical floor plan – an oblong prayer-hall wider than it was deep – derived from the Great Ommayad Mosque in Damascus, the model *par excellence* for such buildings.

One such building was the Ulu Camii (Great Mosque) of Diyarbakır, whose construction is thought to date from the eighth century, and thus predates the Turkish period. It was, however, substantially rebuilt after 1091. As at Damascus, there is re-use of classical *spolia* such as columns, Corinthian capitals, key-patterns, and vine and *cantharus* friezes. Before the huge prayer-hall stands a porticoed courtyard, also wider than it is deep.

The freestone in which all these buildings are constructed is of local origin, and was used by the Greeks, Romans and Byzantines before the Muslim architects. It is also characteristic of the Selçuk period.

Certain buildings dating from the first decades of the Turkish occupation of Anatolia still bear an Arabic imprint. These are the great mosques of Mardin, Dunaysir (modern Kızıltepe) and Sivas, and a part of the Alaeddin Camii at Konya; in all these buildings, the oblong plan testifies to the continuity of classical tradition in Islamic prayer-halls.

These mosques, with their hypostyle plan divided into aisles and bays, strongly influenced the earliest Selçuk buildings in Anatolia. An example of the latter is the prayer-hall of the Alaeddin Camii in Niğde (1223). It has three aisles, and its *mihrab*

The Elements of the Mosque

Muslim prayer

The mosque is where Muslims meet to pray. The Koran prescribes five prayers daily, which are accompanied by ritual prostration in the direction of the Kaaba in Mecca. For this reason, all mosques are orientated towards the Kaaba. This direction is shown by the *mihrab*, a niche in the *qibla* wall. To the right of the *mihrab* stands the *minbar*, a raised pulpit from which the preacher addresses the faithful.

The buildings devoted to prayer in Islam have taken different forms in different parts of the Muslim world.

The faithful are summoned to prayer five times a day by the voice of the *muezzin* sounding from the top of the minaret. The devotee must face Mecca, where the Kaaba or Black Stone is kept; this is the goal of the pilgrimage prescribed by the Law (*umma*). Mecca constitutes the central point of Islam as instituted by Mohammed. On it the thoughts of all Muslims are centred.

Orientation is therefore a significant part of ritual. The direction of Mecca is indicated by the *mihrab*: a niche constructed in the *qibla*, the prayer-hall wall running at right-angles to an imaginary line drawn between it and the Kaaba.

To the right of the *mihrab* stands the *minbar*, a high pulpit reached by stairs; from the *minbar*, the *imam* preaches to the assembled company. In large mosques, a rostrum called the *dikka* is reserved for the *imam*'s assistant, whom the congregation can follow in the ritual gestures and prostrations, making it easier for a large number to take part in common prayer.

In hypostyle mosques, the gates can be either parallel or at right-angles to the *qibla*; the roofed space defines the *haram*, that is, the area devoted to prayer.

In general, the *haram* is reached through a courtyard. This is provided with a fountain or pool for ritual ablution (*sebil* or *şadırvan*). The courtyard mosque originated in Iran and is also found in Selçuk and Mamluk regions. It fre-

quently possesses high vaulted niches on the inside of the courtyard; these are called *iwans* and are generally paired face to face on the two axes of the building. The *pishtaq*, finally, is a large portal at the main point of access to the mosque.

The *madrasa* or religious school, for the most part, exhibits the same components as the mosque, and, in particular, observes the same orientation; its main hall or *iwan* serves as prayer-hall and boasts a *mihrab*.

The Ulu Camii of Diyarbakır
This venerable mosque in eastern Anatolia (above) dates from the eighth century. From 1091 on, it was much modified by Turkish architects. But its plan clearly derives from the Great Ommayad Mosque in Damascus. A further point of resemblance is its reuse of classical elements (below): columns, capitals, and vine-leaf mouldings. It is one of the oldest Islamic monuments in Anatolia.

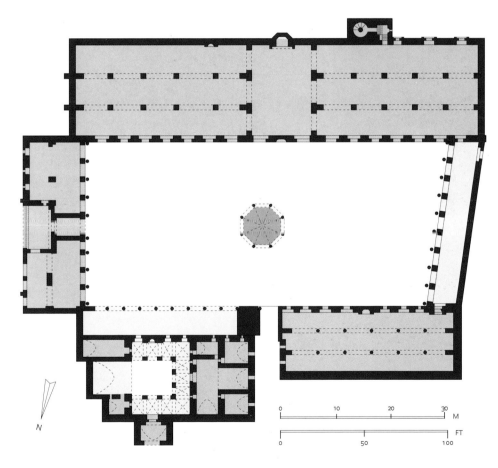

A classical plan
The oblong plan of the mosque at Diyarbakır: its three bays on either side of a short central nave, and its huge courtyard, all derive from the pre-eminent model, that of the Great Ommayad Mosque at Damascus, which was built in 715.

is preceded by a dome on squinches flanked by two smaller domes. Its four bays are covered with slightly pointed ribbed vaults. A central opening, forming a light-well, illuminates the interior. This arrangement is also found in the Huant Hatun Camii, in Kayseri, which dates from 1237. The latter is a much larger building (56 by 50 m) with eight aisles and ten bays; eighty-four shafts carry the massive arcades, which run perpendicular to the *qibla*. The *mihrab* is preceded by a large dome.

The hypostyle formula with light-well is also found in a building that shares with the Afyon mosque the distinction of following a still earlier plan. This is the Eşrefoğlu Camii at Beyşehir, on the shores of the lake of the same name in western Anatolia. It dates from 1296, and exhibits within its stone structure a forest of wooden columns, which support a flat timber roof. Capitals adorned with stalactite work ornament the long slender columns, which form seven naves and nine bays.

Though hypostyle prayer-halls manifest the influence of classical Arab mosques, particularly in their plans, they also present specifically Selçuk characteristics. Thus the façade of the Alaeddin Camii in Konya, completed in 1220, possesses a fine portal decorated with the polychrome marbles typical of Rum Selçuk art.

The portal displays superlative interlaced arch motifs surrounding a tympanum with slightly pointed arch and colonnettes with zig-zag grooves; the plat-band with

A vaulted prayer-hall
A series of slightly pointed barrel vaults resting on short pillars and supported by four-centred arches covers the prayer-hall of the Alaeddin Camii at Niğde. The carpets on the floor assist ritual prostration.

Plan of the Alaeddin Camii
Rectangular in plan, the prayer-hall comprises three aisles and five bays, and is entered via a door on one side. The arches bearing its vaulted ceiling spring from eight square pillars, while the bay preceding the *mihrab* is roofed by three domes, one of which is a domical vault comprising eight webs.

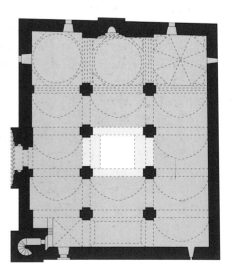

Left
An arcaded prayer-hall
The Huant Hatun Camii, at Kayseri, dates from 1237. Its vast prayer-hall is rectangular in plan and comprises eight aisles and ten bays. In the centre, a light-well precedes the domed space in front of the *mihrab*. Slightly pointed arches provide the wind-bracing.

Right
A composition of *muqarnas*
The portal of the Huant Hatun Camii at Kayseri is surmounted by a stalactite niche whose geometrical design disguises its structural function.

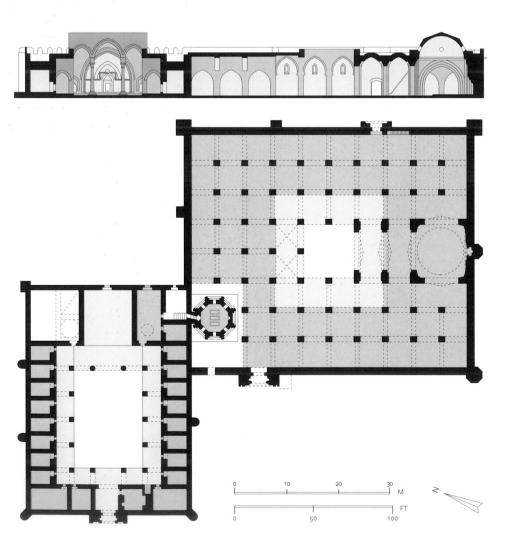

The Huant Hatun complex at Kayseri
Longitudinal section and plan: to the left, the courtyard *madrasa*; to the right the mosque. A handsome octagonal *türbe* stands at the junction of the two buildings. The eight aisles and ten bays of the prayer-hall are roofed with vaults resting on forty-eight square pillars, which are replaced by massive piers in the domed space in front of the *mihrab*. The section illustrates the variety of roofing techniques employed.

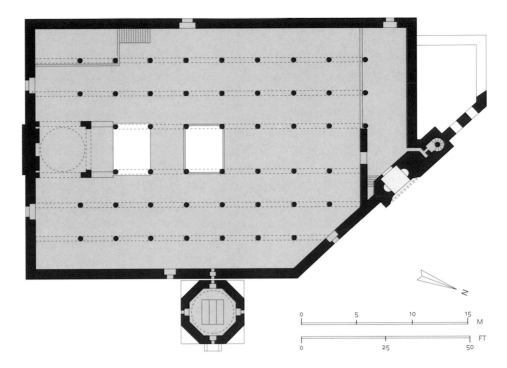

The Eşrefoğlu Camii
The mosque of Eşrefoğlu at Beyşehir dates from 1298. Its seven aisles and nine bays form a rectangle, one corner of which has been cut off to form the entrance. Inside, some fifty handsome wooden columns with stalactite capitals carry the flat timber roof. There are two light-wells in front of the *mihrab*. A *türbe* set against one of the side walls completes the complex.

alternated voussoirs serves to divert the load from the lintel. These features constitute a decorative style soon to be adopted for both the *madrasas* and the caravanserais of the thirteenth century. The gateway of the Alaeddin Camii in Konya is a very early example, somewhat restrained in style, but a more highly developed form of this ornamentation is found in many buildings in Cappadocia.

One such building is the Büyük Karatay Medresesi in Konya, which was founded in 1251. The portal that precedes the domed prayer-hall adopts an ornamental idiom similar to that of the Alaeddin Camii, but enriches it with a stalactite tympanum. This honeycomb vaulting transposes into stone a formula developed by the Great Selçuks of Isfahan in Persia.

Built a century before, the Isfahan monuments possess honeycomb structures that attained quite large dimensions during the early development of the style. By their reciprocal buttressing they formed the vaults of the courtyard *iwans*. When the honeycomb effect was reduced in scale, the stalactites lost all structural functions and became purely ornamental. But this so-called *muqarna* style thereafter became one of the recurrent themes of Persian, Arab and Turkish Islamic art.

Another element of Persian origin is evident in Rum Selçuk architecture: the glazed bricks that adorn parts of the building, especially the door and *mihrab*. The Şifaiye Medresesi (in this case a hospital) in Sivas, dating from 1217, is a particularly good example. There the *iwan* that precedes the *türbe* or mausoleum of Keykavus is ornamented with turquoise blue.

The origin of this polychrome style was in the glazed bricks produced in Kashan in south-west Persia. The Arab authors of the tenth century refer to the use of a blue glaze on the inside of the domes of Baghdad. This colour was obtained by mixing cobalt, sulphur and arsenic. In Selçuk architecture, polychrome tiles were frequently used to decorate the *mihrab*. The city of Kashan exported its production far and wide during the eleventh and twelfth centuries, for a long time keeping the technique for manufacturing its ceramics a secret. The glazed bricks, black or blue, possessed a metallic iridescence imparted by the gaseous oxides formed in the oven during vitrification. Decorations made up of octagonal or star-shaped *kashis* (Kashan bricks) were used in palaces or pavilions, and could be assembled

Stalactite capitals

The wooden capitals of the
Eşrefoğlu Camii illustrate how
Selçuk architecture, a product
of the remote areas whence the
Turkish tribes originated, came
to absorb the conventions of
the Islamic tradition.

Wooden columns

The tall, elegant columns which
carry the roof of the Eşrefoğlu
Camii at Beyşehir. The mosque
exemplifies an archaic form of
prayer-hall unique to the Selçuks
of Anatolia. Its model would seem
to be the prototypical works of
Middle Eastern architecture,
the *apadana* (hypostyle halls)
of the Achaemenids, Hittites,
Medes and Urarteans.

to form human or animal figures. Their use indicates that the prohibition on the representation of living beings within Islam was effectively confined to prayer-halls.

Polychrome tiles are found in the Büyük Karatay Medresesi of Konya, whose dome, lit by an oculus directly above the pool provided for ablutions, is supported on Turkish triangles with a revetment of black and blue tiles. We should note that the term "Turkish triangles" refers to an architectural formula originating with the Rum Selçuks; it solves the problem raised by the transition from a square plan building to the circular base of a dome. The medieval Turks used neither of the two classic solutions that had been in use since Roman times, that is: the squinch (corner arch) and pendentive (triangle in spherical profile). Instead they used a triangular surface with rectilinear sides. The Turkish triangle provides a stereometrically satisfying junction between an orthogonal and a circular plan.

The use of an oculus at the apex of the dome to illuminate the internal space of the *madrasa* is taken directly from the conventional formula of Roman bath com-

Left
Polychrome masonry
A detail of the arch above the portal of the Alaeddin Camii in Konya, which was finished in 1220. Dark and light stone is alternated in the voussoirs, which are positioned to match the interlacing arches above them. The same device features in the lintel course. The lintel itself carries an ornamental carving in Turkish and is set in a carved frame decorated with *muqarnas*.

Right
A derivative ornamental vocabulary
Selçuk ornamentation adapted classical models to the new language of Islam. Here the capital derives from the Corinthian style, while the zig-zag takes its inspiration from "salomonic" columns.

Classical *spolia*
The façade of the Alaeddin Camii in Konya. To the right and left of the great portal with its geometric motifs in polychrome stone are a series of bays forming an ornamental frieze; they make use of blocks of stone from Byzantine buildings.

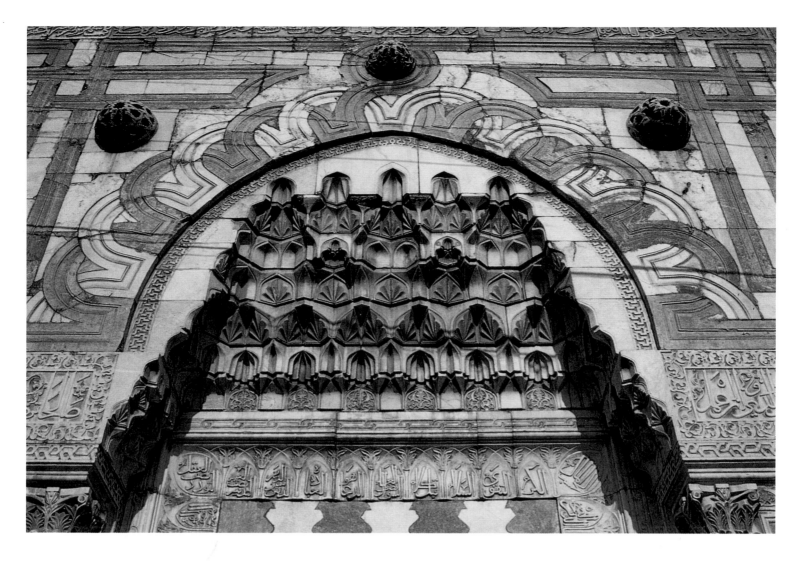

A façade of stalactites
The Büyük Karatay Medresesi
in Konya dates from 1251. Its
portal copies the interlaced voussoirs of the Alaeddin Camii, but
the polychrome tympanum
is replaced by a fine display of
low-relief stalactites.

Ceramic mosaics
The *madrasa* is illuminated by
an oculus set in a dome whose
intrados is covered in ceramic
star motifs. The Turkish triangles
provide the transition from the
square plan to the circular base
of the dome, and have a similar
ceramic revetment.

A polychrome ceramic *mihrab*
At Ankara, the Selçuk Arslanhane Camii is thought to have been built by the Emir Sayfeddin. The fine stalactite *mihrab* is enhanced by the use of blue-glazed brick and dates from 1289. The *muqarna* work is of exceptionally refined geometrical design.

plexes. Examples of these had no doubt survived in Konya among the ruins of ancient Iconium. The minaret (now ruinous) of the İnce Minare Medresesi of Konya, which was built in 1260–1265, makes particularly interesting use of glazed brick. To the right of the splendid sculpted portal of this domed *madrasa*, the minaret, which was once extremely tall, is now reduced to only two levels, a third storey having collapsed in earthquakes early in the twentieth century. The first level is stone-built and square in plan, and supports a cylindrical second level of brick, on which are *tori* covered in green tiling; on these, green and black lozenge motifs are pricked out to form a stylised lettering that spells the name of Allah.

The portal of the İnce Minare Medresesi is one of the most audacious attempts ever undertaken to combine the sacred text of the Koran with ornamental formulas. It overflows with ornamental framing, tracery and floral motifs. This rich decoration is set in an almost baroque composition, in which the inscribed mouldings framing the portal intertwine like ribbons, extend to its summit and from there fall back along its edges.

It is an extraordinary achievement, in which an artist has sought to reinterpret the standard formula of the *pishtaq*, the great rectangular portal of Persian origin.

Asymmetrical symmetry

The İnce Minare Medresesi at Konya dates from 1265. The square central hall is reached via a vestibule, and is roofed with a dome on Turkish triangles at whose centre is an oculus, as in the Büyük Karatay Medresesi. The large axial *iwan* is flanked by two smaller domed rooms, in which the domes are carried on Turkish pleats.

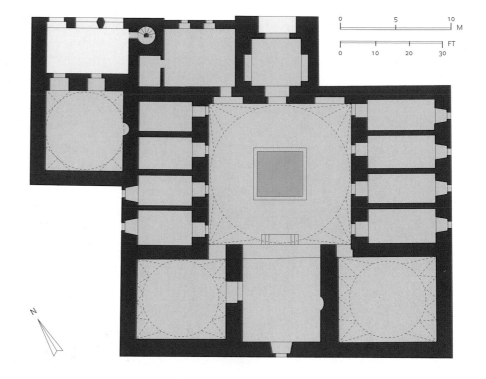

A handsome façade

The façade includes a superlative *pishtaq*; its abundant decoration mixes epigraphic string-courses and floral and geometric motifs. To its right, the "slender minaret" after which the *madrasa* is named exhibits a pioneering combination of carved stone and polychrome tiles. The third section of the minaret fell during an earthquake around the turn of the century.

Fertility of invention
A plant motif (left) from the corner of the İnce Minare Medresesi at Konya stands in stark contrast to the geometrical tracery from the same portal (right). Selçuk ornamental carving makes a mockery of stylistic distinctions.

Juxtaposition and contrast
A further detail from the *pishtaq*. On the corner, an openwork knot stands out against a floral band, itself contrasted with the geometrical moulding that frames an ornamental inscription. The eclecticism of Selçuk architecture is exemplified in these unexpected juxtapositions.

But the Turkish artist has radically modified the Persian design. A formula derived from ceramic decoration is transformed by the use of carved stone; for the play of colour in polychrome tiling is substituted the play of light in the intricate relief of the stone portal.

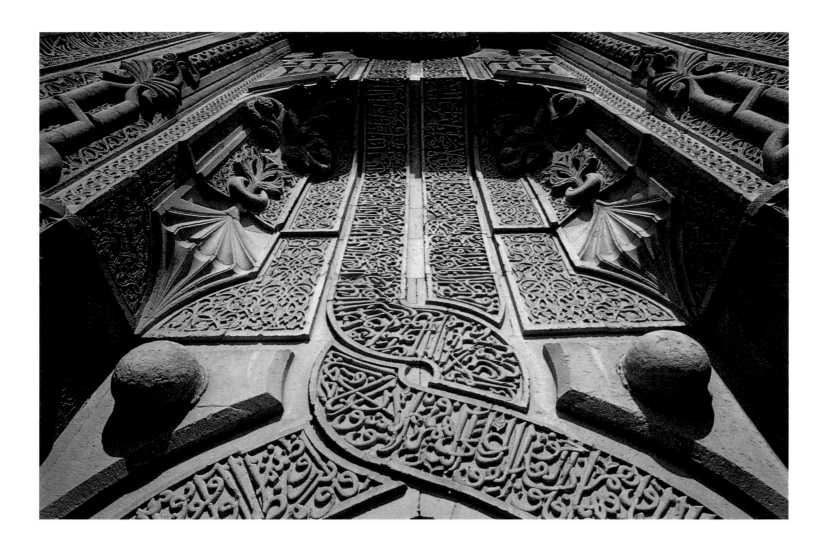

Authoritative originality

This view up the face of the portal of the İnce Minare Medresesi at Konya reveals the exuberance of the Selçuk ornamental vocabulary of the thirteenth century. The decoration of the *pishtaq* plays off plant against geometrical motifs and floral bands against inscriptions, juxtaposing intricate low-relief carving with smooth projecting forms.

Aspects and Function of the *madrasa*

We have already mentioned several Selçuk *madrasas*. For the Turks, the construction of Koranic schools was part of a policy of propagating the return to Sunni orthodoxy, which had been challenged by the Shiite Fatimids. In terms of Islamic doctrine, the *madrasa* is the equivalent of the *ghazi*, the soldiers whose faith leads them to volunteer for service on the frontiers, or wherever the struggle with Christianity takes them.

The great profusion of Selçuk *madrasas* was produced by this campaigning orthodoxy, and a desire to ensure that Islam retained its pure and original form. For this reason, each Anatolian town possessed at least one such Koranic school. A similar attitude prevailed in Persia and other Great Selçuk territories. In the *madrasas*, the masters set out the principles of Islam. Theological studies included juridical matters, since the Koran was the source of both theological doctrine and the rules of everyday life. It constituted the Law as set out by the *ulamas* (doctors), the *qadis* (judges) and *muftis* (legal experts). The official doctrines were embraced by a variety of different schools of thought, notably the Hanifis, the Hanbalis, the Shafi'is and the Malikis.

During the Rum Selçuk era, the *madrasa* underwent a dramatic development. As standard-bearers of the Prophet, *madrasas* affirmed the faith; in their construction no expense was too great and no embellishment too lavish. *Madrasa* architects could thus adopt the large-scale formulas required to provide for a series of complementary functions.

The Çifte Minare Medresesi at Erzurum on the river Aras, built in 1253, exemplifies this. Its powerful structure consists of a porticoed courtyard, two high minarets faced with glazed brick, and a *türbe*: that is, a tomb with a conical roof.

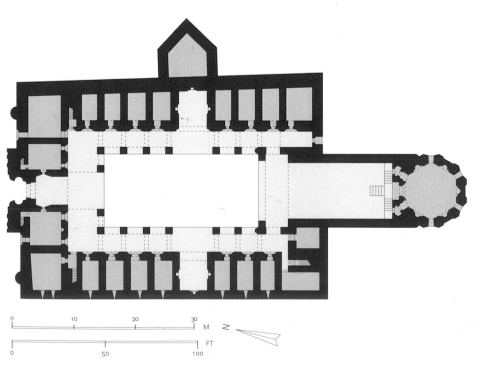

Above and page 39

An impressive façade

On the high Anatolian plateau, at Erzurum, stands the Çifte Minare Medresesi, built in 1253. Its symmetrical façade is surmounted by two fluted minarets in glazed brick, from which the building takes its name. The structure of the right-hand minaret was unsettled by earthquakes.

A porticoed courtyard

The plan of the Çifte Minare Medresesi in Erzurum combines a courtyard comprising four axial *iwans* in the Persian manner with a large dodecagonal *türbe*; the latter forms an axial extension of the principal *iwan*. The rooms of the teachers and assistants are set around the courtyard on two storeys.

Decorative interlace in stone
On either side of the portal of the Çifte Minare Medresesi, stalactite niches offer a series of interwoven motifs sculpted in *champlevé* technique. The columns and capitals almost disappear under the abundant floral decoration.

Exuberance and sobriety
There is little or no regularity in the decoration of the courtyard portico. A column with interlace motifs is followed by a plain column, in turn followed by an octagonal one whose facets are covered in repeated motifs.

The porticoed courtyard
Behind its pointed four-centred arch, the courtyard of the Çifte Minare Medresesi in Erzurum presents its two-storey portico; in the background are the two brick minarets that flank the entrance.

Two-storey arcading
The rhythm of the columns and pointed arches surrounding the courtyard is emphasised by the majestic axial *iwans*. At ground-floor level, tie-beams ensure the stability of the arcades.

The Hatuniye Türbesi
The Selçuk tomb or *türbe* lends itself to an expansive decorative repertory. The Hatuniye Türbesi at Erzurum dates from 1255. Under its conical roof are several different kinds of frieze, while cord-mouldings outline the arches defining each of its eight sides.

A monumental tomb
The Hatuniye Türbesi was built by the daughter of the Sultan Alaeddin Keykubad in memory of her father, who died in 1237 at Kayseri. It is inspired by Persian tower tombs, which were generally built in brick; here the rubblestone walls are faced with ashlar.

The Yivli Minare
In southern Anatolia, in the coastal town of Antalya, a superb brick minaret was built alongside a Byzantine church that had been converted into a mosque. The Yivli Minare was constructed by Keykubad I and dates from 1230. Its elegantly fluted form rises out of an octagon set on a square base.

Erzurum, in eastern Anatolia, was an important transit stage for caravan traffic, and the *madrasa* stands on the edge of the city, 1800 m above the desert landscape. Its dimensions are imposing. It is 75 m long and 25 m wide; its central courtyard measures 25 by 12 m, and possesses two pairs of facing *iwans*, like those of Persian mosques and *madrasas*.

The fine portal takes the form of a *pishtaq*, and possesses a niche of honeycomb stalactites. Over it stand two tall brick minarets. The portal gives on to a courtyard bordered by two levels of porticoes whose arcades are supported by columns. In the middle of each of the inner façades of the courtyard, the *iwans* form high bays, whose pointed arches rise two storeys in a single sweep. The decoration sculpted in the dark trachyte stone enlivens the surfaces of the octagonal and round columns with geometrical and floral motifs.

The culminating element of the complex is the sturdy mausoleum, the Hatuniye Türbesi; the massive dodecagon of the funerary chamber is capped with a high conical roof. Bands of superlative interlace and corded motifs ornament the roof.

The combination of *madrasa* and *türbe* was quite common; it appears in Kayseri in the Huant Hatun complex, which dates from 1237, and the Köşk Medrese of 1339. The resulting complexes united the orthogonal structure traditional in mosques and *madrasas* with the cylindrical and conical elements of the mausoleum.

Among the monuments of Sivas – an important centre of Selçuk art – we have already mentioned the Şifaiye, the hospital of Keykavus, which dates from 1217, and its *iwan* decorated with glazed motifs. The plan of this building, whose porticoes are reflected in a central pool of water, constituted the prototype for many of the large Selçuk *madrasas*. The number of students coming forward required that the formula

used in Konya – a teaching room covered by one or more domes (as in the İnce Minare Medresesi and Büyük Karatay Medresesi) – give way to one that could accommodate a greater number. This was the Persian-style courtyard mosque, generally with four *iwans*; it gradually came to predominate.

The fact that hospitals, *khanqahs* (monasteries for dervishes, that is, mendicant monks), *nizamiyas* (colleges of theological and scientific studies), and *madrasas* all exhibited the same plan, with central courtyard and *iwans*, testifies to the religious and social programme implemented by the sultans. The Selçuk and Ottoman creation of soup-kitchens for the poor, dispensaries, alms-houses and schools reflects the piety of the sultans and their respect for the charitable obligations prescribed by the Koran. They took every opportunity to demonstrate their generosity through charitable foundations, to which they gave their names. Inscriptions commemorate these inalienable donations, whose charters tended to provide for their "perpetual" upkeep.

An Aesthetic Language

The development of the *madrasa* towards ever more emphatic monumentality is well illustrated by the examples built in Sivas. We have noted one outstanding example of this development in the Çifte Minare Medresesi in Erzurum. Another is the Çifte Minare Medresesi in Sivas. Built in 1271, it shows a particularly luxuriant decoration; like the Çifte Minare in Erzurum it has a large axial gateway flanked by two minarets. Unfortunately, only the splendid gateway survives. The combination of limestone and marble ashlar blocks with polychrome brick minarets provided a satisfactory solution to the technical problems posed by building on this scale. As in Konya, the minarets have corbelled upper galleries.

This combination of stone and polychrome brick was first used in Selçuk Persia. It allows for organic development of great architectural power, conferring on the *madrasa* an imposing and symbolic character. Its treatment at Sivas, with the *pish-taq* portal flanked by a pair of minarets, is highly successful.

The tomb of a great sultan
In Sivas, Sultan Keykavus (1211–1220) constructed a hospital in 1217. This was later converted into the Şifaiye Medresesi. Here stands the sovereign's *türbe*, built behind an *iwan* (below). Its presence is signalled by the blue ceramic inscription (above).

Right

An imposing façade

The Gök Medrese in Sivas. At the centre of the symmetrical façade is a superb stone portal whose niche is profusely ornamented with stalactites. The two brick minarets have corbelled galleries carried by rows of *muqarnas*.

Left

Exuberant carving at Sivas

In the Selçuk monuments of Sivas, a highly ornate style prevails, and the most diverse motifs are found side by side. A detail from the portal of the Gök Medrese, built in 1271.

The Gök Medrese ("Blue Medrese") in Sivas also dates from 1271 and borrows the same formula. It is a fine illustration of the ornamentation of Anatolian Selçuk portals. Within the framework created by its successive vertical borders, intricately incised with tracery and floral motifs, and the *muqarna* "friezes", the doorway itself stands in a niche whose vault is dense with stalactite work. The wide-shouldered ogee arch that frames this *iwan* is supported by slender engaged columns of bonded stone; their capitals are of Corinthian derivation.

At the crest of the portal, three curious, almost baroque decorative elements proffer their floral designs. Like those of the Great Mosque in Divriği, they seem to be stone engravings of motifs derived from polychrome ceramics. The portal of the Muzaffer Bürüciye Medresesi (1271) in Sivas is studded with these high-relief designs. It belongs to a period contemporary with the Mongol Ilkhan dynasty, when Sivas enjoyed a period of intense architectural creativity. On either side of the great axial *iwan*, graceful arcades supported by columns form porticoes, which open on to

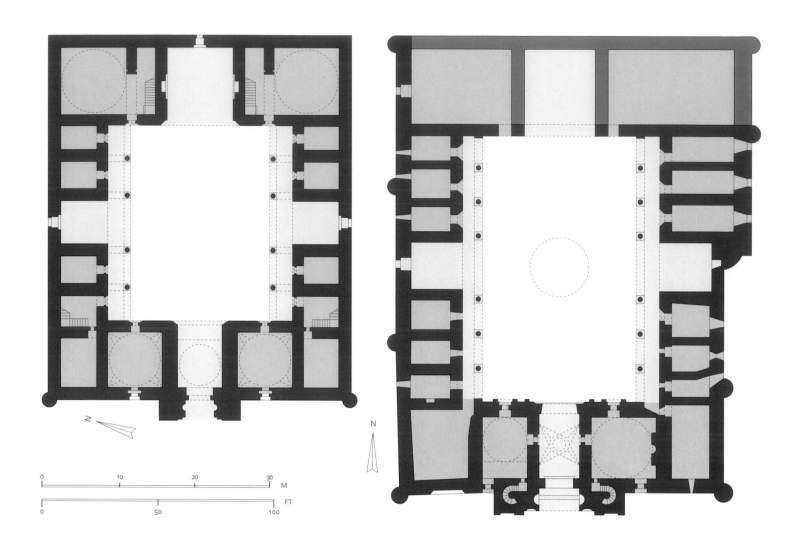

Madrasas with four *iwans*
The plans of the Muzaffer Bürüciye Medresesi (left) and Gök Medrese (right), both in Sivas, show a clear Persian influence; each is built around a courtyard dominated by the *iwans* set on the four axes of the building.

Courtyard arcades
In the Muzaffer Bürüciye Medresesi, the lateral *iwan* is distinguished only by the extra width of its pointed arch and the recess behind it; it stands on one of the building's four axes.

A Turkish "baroque"

In the portal of the Muzaffer Bürüciye Medresesi in Sivas, the stalactite niche is set into a surface alive with floral motifs beneath a superb limestone platband carved with inscriptions. The four strange projecting elements are exquisitely carved with floral motifs; their shadows animate the busy surface behind them.

A *pishtaq* portal

The overall view of the portal of the Muzaffer Bürüciye Medresesi clearly shows how the doorway is framed. Its decoration exemplifies that of Selçuk buildings in Anatolia. In the centre, the door to the central courtyard opens under a depressed arch with alternating voussoirs.

Carved motifs
These three details from the portal of the Çifte Minare Medresesi in Sivas show the exquisite openwork motifs (above left), the profusion of interlace and floral motifs (above right), the juxtaposition of different framing devices and free versions of the Corinthian capital (below).

Page 48
The Çifte Minare portal
In common with many of the principal buildings of the city, the Çifte Minare Medresesi in Sivas is the work of a Mongol Governor who represented the Ilkhanid dynasty. The presence of the Mongols seems to have had little effect on the evolution of the Rum Selçuk style of the late thirteenth century. Here, beneath two minarets in polychrome glazed brick, the form of the portal is emphasised by the powerful *muqarna* framing.

the rooms of the masters and students. A larger arch on either side marks the presence of the lateral *iwans*, where teaching took place.

The teeming splendour of Selçuk ornamentation contrasts strongly with the bare walls on which it is inscribed, and this is one of the distinguishing marks of Anatolian art: the decoration is confined to certain areas of the building. Its role is to enhance the more important components of the building: the portal, the *iwan*, columns, and other elements, enriching them with its very diverse ornamental vocabulary.

Subtle carving
The Döner Kümbet in Kayseri dates from 1275 and exhibits the same mixture of stalactite and floral decoration as the Hatuniye Türbesi at Erzurum (see page 42).

Dodecagonal *türbe*
The Döner Kümbet is dedicated to the Princess Şah Cihan Hatun. It rests on a square base whose cut-away corners link it to the dodecagonal base of the chamber walls. The roof is conical.

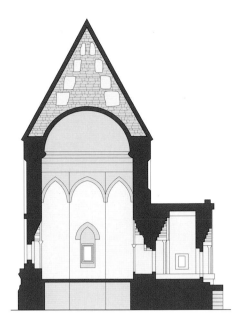

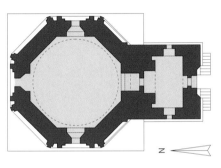

A projecting vestibule
Section and plan of the Ali Cafer *türbe* at Kayseri, a late work of the mid-fourteenth century, octagonal in plan; under the roof, a dome of semicircular section forms the ceiling of the funerary chamber, which is preceded by a vestibule.

A Karaman mausoleum
At the foot of the Taurus mountains, the city of Karaman was the capital of an Emirate during the thirteenth and fourteenth centuries. In this oasis stands the very austere *türbe* of Karamanoğlu Alaeddin Bey.

The *türbe* or Mausoleum

We have already mentioned the *türbe*, the cylindrical or polygonal Turkish mausoleum with its conical roof. This was the highly geometrical form chosen by the Selçuks in Anatolia for funerary monuments. The origin of Islamic mausoleums is to be found at Samarra, in present-day Iraq, where in 862 the tomb of the Caliph al-Mustanzir was built. The custom of designating the tomb of a notable by the construction of a commemorative building quickly spread throughout Persia; there it accompanied the rise of Shiite Islam, since the Shiites venerate the tombs of the imams and of their direct descendants, the Immazadeh, who were considered the only true heirs to the Prophet.

In northern Persia, the Ziyarid dynasty built one of the first monumental tombs in the form of a tower, the mausoleum of Gunbad-i-Qabus, at Gorgan, not far from the Caspian Sea; it dates from 1006. In plan, it is a star-shaped polygon with prom-

A late Karamanid work
The Hudavent Hatun Türbesi
at Niğde is a highly original work
dating from 1312; it was built by
the daughter of Sultan Rukeddin
Kılıçarslan IV. Its undercut base,
supported by stalactite corbels,
carries an octagonal building.
Muqarna canopies project at each
corner in the form of external
squinches.

inent corners and a conical roof. This was the model for the Turkish *türbe*, in which
stone replaced the brick used in Persia.

The quest for an austere geometrical form to signal the metaphysical aspect of
the tomb is particularly clear in the Döner Kümbet (1275) and the Ali Cafer Kümbeti,
both at Kayseri. The *türbes* of Hudavent Hatun (1312) at Niğde and Halime Hatun at
Gevaş (1358), both of which date from the Karamanid Emirate, exemplify this aspiration to a bare, sculptural quality, which does not exclude a wealth of remarkable
decoration. The decoration of friezes, bands of inscriptions, engaged colonnettes,
rosettes and stalactites continues the Selçuk tradition.

A proper assessment of Rum Selçuk achievement in architecture must acknow-
ledge the considerable debt that it owed to the two distinct traditions we have
examined. The first was the Arab heritage of Islamic forms and spaces. The second
was the influence of the Great Selçuks of Persia, who maintained almost continuous
contact with the Rum Selçuk state.

An unusual solution
A detail of the *türbe* of Hudavent Hatun at Niğde, showing the *muqarna* projections at the corners of the building; geometrical and plant motifs alternate in the decoration.

Christian influences
Above an openwork window of the Hudavent Hatun Türbesi, the two birds carved in relief show a striking relation to Armenian carvings, and in particular to the decoration of the Church of the Holy Cross on Akhtamar Island in Lake Van.

The Caravan Routes

The Anatolian Staging-Posts

Page 55
Decoration of a fortified caravanserai
The Selçuk caravanserais of Anatolia often possess sumptuous portals decorated with geometrical motifs. Here, stalactites form a vigorous framing device in the entrance to the Sultanhanı near Aksaray (1229).

Angle tower of a fortified caravanserai
With its alternating courses of light and dark stone (*ablaq* work), the outer wall of the Sadeddin Han is a fine example of the defensive architecture developed for the Selçuk caravanserais. It stands in the middle of the Anatolian steppe and was built in 1235–1236.

For the inhabitant or traveller in central Anatolia during the Rum Selçuk period, security was a major concern. In spite of being a Rum Selçuk possession, between the late eleventh and thirteenth centuries the region was variously overrun by Byzantine troops, Crusaders, and the Mongol hordes. Towns were surrounded by powerful fortifications intended to protect families and their goods. The protection of trade and travellers in the high plateaux between Persia and the Aegean, or the Black Sea and the Mediterranean, was secured by a succession of fortified caravanserais.

Heirs to the Romano-Byzantine arts of siege and defence, the Turks restored and improved the fortifications of the cities that they occupied in Asia Minor. The best example of this is Kayseri (the Roman Caesarea) in Cappadocia. Because it was a commercial hub of central Anatolia, Kayseri's defences were reinforced with a new city wall, and a citadel in the centre, built over the foundations of Justinian's citadel, with nineteen towers of dark basalt. The square towers projecting from the curtain walls give Kayseri, even today, an impregnable air.

From documents we know of the circular wall of Konya (Iconium), which Hadrian had made a Roman settlement. It became the capital of the Selçuks in 1097, and in 1221 Keykubad I (1221–1237) surrounded it with a city wall furnished with 144 towers. No trace of it remains today. By contrast, other fortified cities, such as Diyarbakır on the Tigris, still possess their imposing city walls, in which elements of Byzantine and Selçuk construction survive intermingled.

Along the Caravan Trail

We have already noted the importance of international trade to the sultans, and the role played by the trans-Anatolian routes, along which goods from the Orient were transported from the Black Sea to the Mediterranean without passing through the Byzantine-held Bosphorus Straits. (The caravans used the camels of the steppe, which were more resistant to cold than the North African or Arabian dromedaries.) The building of these roads required close attention from the sultans. They were, for the most part, Roman roads, which had to be repaired; the ruinous monuments and works of art to be found along them also had to be restored, and safe refuges built at regular intervals.

The sultans set about a huge bridge-building programme, and some of its results still survive. One such is the bridge over the river Köprüçay (known to the Greeks as the Eurymedon) near Aspendus. It has withstood the ravages of time magnificently; its four great pointed arches stride across the river carrying a road that rises up towards the centre.

The caravan routes were tracks intended not for carts but for camels, and therefore required a metalled surface only in places. There were two main axes: east to west, between the Persian border and the Aegean, and north to south, joining Samsun to Kayseri. From there, the route followed the great valley between Kayseri and Konya, Beyşehir and Eğirdir, before descending through the Taurus to Antalya.

Military architecture
The citadel of Kayseri replaced the Roman and Byzantine fortresses of Caesarea. It was built in *circa* 1224 by Keykavus and is one of the finest surviving Selçuk military complexes in Anatolia.

Roads and bridges
This Selçuk bridge with its elegant, slightly pointed arches spans the Köprüçay river (known to the Greeks as the Eurymedon) in Pamphylia. The sultans made every effort to secure communications, building fortified caravanserais along the military and commercial routes.

Page 59

An impressive citadel
The city wall of Kayseri stands at the foot of the volcano, Mount Erciyes, which dominates the city. The line of the walls follows that of Justinian's citadel. The dark basalt renders the square, crenellated towers and advance scarp still more formidable.

A Selçuk caravanserai
The Sadeddin Han stands in the middle of the Anatolian steppe. It is unusual to find the portal of a caravanserai in the long side of the rectangular courtyard, as here. Its alternating courses of dark and light stone exemplify the splendour of the Selçuk caravanserais. The motives of the Selçuk sultans are clear; their prosperity depended on international commerce.

There were other routes that performed the same function: for example, the Aksaray-Niğde-Adana road, and another between Beyşehir and Alanya. The result was the construction of around a hundred caravanserais, of which a certain number are still intact.

The Silk and Slave Trades

These were strategic trade and military routes. In time of war, the caravanserais became garrisoned arms depots. Along these routes came a considerable share of the international trade from China and central Asia. The southern trade route came by the oasis of Turfan, down the valley of the Ferghana, across the Turkoman steppe and the Caspian Sea to the shores of the Black Sea.

Down the "Silk Road", through the Khyber and Kandahar passes came the products of India, Indo-China and the islands of what is now Indonesia (spices, ivory and cloth), reaching Anatolia via Balkh and Bukhara. And there was trade, too, from the north, in particular furs from Siberia, which were used in court rituals.

But much of the trade was in slaves from Khirgizia and Kazakhstan, between Lake Balkash and the Syr-Dar'ya, or from the Kipchak plains between the Volga and Danube basins. These Turkic peoples provided the contingents of soldier-slaves whom the Selçuks sold on to their rich southern clients. Redoubtable warriors, they formed the guard of the Caliphs of Baghdad and of the Ayyubids of Damascus.

From these slaves arose the Mamluk dynasties of Cairo and the sultans of Delhi. They were the pillars on which rested the power of several Muslim regimes, and they played a major role in the series of confrontations that took place in the Oriental world. The immediate consequence was an increasing demand for these men, who were worth their weight in gold. And the suppliers of these mamluks were, for the most part, the Rum Selçuks, who sent across Anatolia the contingents that they had purchased or captured in the steppes of Asia.

When they arrived in Anatolia, these young captives were given a rigorous military training. They served an apprenticeship in "houses" from which they emerged the bearers of a highly respected title. These soldier-slaves were the true professional soldiers of the Near and Middle East. They thus became the élite of the Islamic armies, so much so that they alone proved capable, in the second half of the thirteenth century, of defeating the Mongol hordes and so checking their advance.

Thus Selçuk Anatolia became a centre of international trade. It was the marketplace for the slave-warriors who built up and destroyed kingdoms and empires. No

Fortress of long-haul commerce
Sadeddin Han is a huge walled rectangle studded with alternate round and square towers; octagonal towers stand at its corners. It was built by Keykubad I in 1235–1236. The splendid stonemasonry, using alternating courses of different heights, exemplifies the importance accorded by the Rum Selçuks to public works.

Sculpture and outline
A detail of the refined but sober ornamentation of the portal. Selçuk architecture is defined by the stonemason's art.

wonder the sultans paid so much attention to these land routes; their investments in infrastructure were highly profitable. As a result, their caravanserais became not just staging-posts, but works of art in themselves.

An Imposing Architecture

The external appearance of the caravanserais – the few remaining examples are to be found in the immense semi-desert expanses of Anatolia – is similar to that of the forts built by the Romans on the *limes* (the frontier with the Germanic tribes). Rectangular buildings, to the outside world they offer nothing but blank walls. There is no opening with the exception of the monumental gateway, and the walls are dotted with square, polygonal or round towers, which mark the corners or interrupt the expanses of curtain wall.

The description certainly applies to the caravanserai (*han*) of Sadeddin, which dates from 1236 and lies in the midst of the steppe to the north-east of Konya. Its two gateways – the outer on the side of the building and the inner at the back of its porticoed courtyard – and the foundations of its angle-towers exhibit alternating courses and voussoirs of pale and grey stone. This polychrome decoration makes up for a certain sobriety in the entrance, which lacks sculpted and stalactite motifs.

Of particular interest are the numerous Roman and Byzantine artefacts to be found in the stonework: funerary steles, sarcophagi, friezes, window jambs and arcades are all incorporated into the caravanserai's façade without aesthetic cohesion. Indeed, sculpted blocks are sometimes set upside down. It seems unlikely that this expresses the triumph of the Turks over the Christian world. More probably these construction materials were at hand, and cheaper than quarrystone. In the bare face of the walls at Sadeddin Han are to be seen a whole series of "signature" marks left by workmen; they seem to derive from Greek or Armenian characters.

Among the several hundred caravanserais catalogued by Kurt Erdmann some thirty years ago, floor plans vary considerably. For the most part, there is a courtyard, behind which stands a covered space called the "winter hall". Winter conditions on the high Anatolian plateaux are very severe, and neither man nor beast could easily survive without shelter.

But these basic elements could be arranged in various ways. Sometimes, lean-to rooms were built against the curtain walls, in accordance with a type common in Per-

Use of *spolia*
The alternating courses of the Sadeddin Han include *spolia*, here visible in the façade of the caravanserai.
Left: Byzantine motifs feature on the sidewall of a sarcophagus: tracery, arches, and a Christian paty cross.
Above right: a Roman funerary stele shows a couple under an *arcosolium*.
Below right: one of the many quarry marks that identify the blocks. Deriving from Greco-Roman rather than Arabic characters, they testify to the origins of the masons who built the Selçuk caravanserais.

A functional monument
Overall view of the Sultanhanı caravanserai, built in 1229 near Aksaray. This is the best conserved of the great Selçuk *hans*. Its outer wall is studded with octagonal and round towers. In the foreground we see the nave of the winter hall with its lantern-tower surmounted by a pyramidal roof. The courtyard projects to the right.

sia. But the Turks of Asia Minor generally preferred a courtyard, which sometimes possessed lateral arcades, and a three- or five-nave hall. The hall generally presented a central nave with side-aisles. Most of the caravanserais were built in regular courses of handsomely dressed stone.

In the most remarkable caravanserais, known as "Sultan Hans", the pointed tunnel vault of the winter hall adopts the depressed or four-centred arch, which is also used for the courtyard arcade and the side-aisles. The main nave, whose vault can be up to 14 m high, has seven bays, in the middle of which is a domed lantern tower. This is round within and octagonal outside, and the point of its conical roof can reach 20 m. The much lower side-aisles (some five metres high) form hypostyle spaces supported by square pillars, and are rather dark.

With its high vault punctuated by transverse ribs, its lateral arcades opening onto the vaulted side-aisles and its central lantern tower, the architecture of the "winter halls" is like that of a church with a pointed barrel vault dominated by a high transept.

The "Sultan Han" caravanserais contributed to the sultans' prosperity and were of more opulent design than the standard building. On their longitudinal axis, the front side of the courtyard has as its façade a large portal with a richly ornamented frame; the access gate is set in a niche dominated by a *muqarna* vault. This sculpted ornament is of fine grained-limestone or pale marble, and is in the same style as the *pishtaqs* of mosques and *madrasas*. These *hans* share the ornamental vocabulary of the religious buildings of Selçuk Anatolia.

The seven arcades of the courtyard, on the left of the portal as one enters, provide much-needed shelter from the blazing summer sun. Opposite, a second portico gives on to apartments and a *hammam* or Turkish bath. In the centre of the open courtyard is a small, raised, cube-shaped building resting on three large arches. This is a little mosque, which is entered by a narrow, steep, double staircase: a place of prayer at the disposal of the passing devotee. Its presence symbolises the fact that the caravanserai as a whole is a work of charity, built by the sultan in compliance with the obligation imposed by the Koran.

A ceremonial gateway

Above left: the monumental *pishtaq* of the Sultanhanı (1229), near Aksaray, with its stalactite niche. *Above right:* a detail of the carved ornamentation of the portal: the zig-zag colonnette imitates "salomonic" columns. Its palm-leaf capital derives from the acanthus motifs of the Corinthian capital.

A functional shelter

The handsome pointed arcades of the courtyard of the Sultanhanı (1232), near Kayseri, have the purity of functional architecture, and are ornamented only by a stalactite frieze.

Provision for prayer
The Ağzi Kara Han was built in 1242 to the east of Aksaray. The cubic building at the centre of the courtyard is a little mosque raised on pointed arches. In the background, the portal of the winter hall.

At the back of the courtyard, a second portal similar to the first, but on a smaller scale, gives access to the winter hall. It too bears sculpted geometric ornamentation, with successive layers of framing and sometimes the same alternation of dark and light courses of stone. As in the mosques and *madrasas*, the decorative repertory is abstract, based on tracery, latticework, star motifs, zig-zags and rosettes, with colonnettes bearing floral capitals. The vault above the inner door, like that of the external portal, is furnished with *muqarnas* of rigorous geometrical precision.

All these features are found in the finest of the Selçuk caravanserais, among which are that built in 1232 on the road that runs north of Kayseri towards Sivas; the Sultanhanı west of Aksaray, which dates from 1229, and is perhaps the finest example, for its state of preservation, restoration, ample size and structural coherence; the Sarıhan, near Avanos, on the course of the river Kızılırmak (known to the Greeks as the Halys), built in the mid-thirteenth century, and recently substantially restored; the Ağzı Kara Hanı of 1242, east of Aksaray, on the Kayseri-Konya road; the Horozlu Han (Han of the Cock) built north-west of Konya around 1246–1249; and finally the Kırkgöz Hanı, built 1236–1246 between Eğirdir and Antalya, with its oblong, single-naved hall at the back of a courtyard flanked by two double porticoes with wide openings that ensure light-filled accommodation.

Each of these buildings shows distinctive and original traits in both plan and decoration. They nevertheless testify to the striking spatial and stylistic unity characteristic of the architecture of the Rum Selçuks.

Selçuk exuberance
The courtyard portal of the Sultanhanı, near Aksaray, exhibits a variety of ornamental motifs. Above the depressed arch with its joggled voussoirs, a band of inscription supports the vigorous stalactites of the niche. The framing of the portal includes successive bands of tracery.

Page 66
Imagination and rigour
Detail of the winter hall portal of the Sultanhanı, north of Kayseri, dating from 1232. In the frame of the *pishtaq*, a geometric knotwork border surrounds the cusp and swastika motifs. Into this panel is set the stalactite niche over the door.

Woven in stone
The ornamental motif surrounding the courtyard gateway of the Sultanhanı (1232), near Kayseri, seems as though woven around the central niche. Rosettes complete the decorative scheme.

A profusion of ornament
Like the portals of the *madrasas*, those of the caravanserais – here, the Sultanhanı – combine a variety of motifs: inscriptions, tracery, *muqarnas*, columns, and polychrome plat-bands.

Structural austerity
In comparison with the exuberant decoration of the portal, the interior of the Sultanhanı (1229), near Aksaray, is austere. The winter hall exhibits arcades of great simplicity; the piers lack capitals and the arches are not decorated. Only the lantern tower interrupts the rhythm of the transverse ribs reinforcing the central barrel vault.

Stalactite squinches
The roof of the Sultanhanı, showing the lantern tower. Under the spiral masonry of the dome are four squinches with stalactite *intrados*.

Clearly defined volumes
Dating from 1246–1249 and standing in the outskirts of Konya, the
Horozlu Han (Han of the Cock)
has a two-level lantern tower
with alternating courses of light
and dark stone; its roof forms an
octagonal pyramid.

A staging-post
On the road linking the Anatolian
plateaux with the shores of the
Mediterranean, the Kırkgöz Hanı,
which dates from 1236–1246, is
the last staging-post before the
port of Antalya. This was the route
for slaves and goods in transit to
Syria and Egypt.

Page 71
Majestic interiors
The winter hall of the Sarıhan
("Yellow Han"), near Avanos,
was built in 1250. It has recently
undergone splendid restoration
and now exemplifies the quality
and coherence of Selçuk caravanserai architecture. The central
section, perpendicular side-aisles
and arcades all display four-
centred arches and barrel vaults.
The lantern tower is the sole
source of light.

From Fontenay to Aksaray
The Cistercian church at Fontenay (left), built in 1139–1147, has a distinctive pointed barrel vault supported by transverse ribs and four-centred lateral barrel vaults. The same features are found in the Turkish caravanserai of Sultanhanı, near Aksaray (right), of 1229.

From le Thoronet to Kayseri
The elegant barrel vault of the nave at le Thoronet (left) dates from 1160–1180. While the use of piers and, in the aisles, quadrant vaulting contrasts with the Cistercian buttressing, the format of the church, with its transverse ribs and three sources of light, is very similar to that of the Sultanhanı, near Kayseri, of 1232 (right).

From l'Escale-Dieu to Avanos
Begun around 1143, the church of l'Escale-Dieu (left) was consecrated in 1160. The pure Cistercian style of the nave and the side-aisle barrel vaults perpendicular to it presages the system adopted for the Sarıhan, near Avanos (right), which was built in 1250 and shares l'Escale-Dieu's austerity.

Domes supported by pendentives

Pointed barrel vaults are one analogy between Christian and Selçuk art; the treatment of domes is another. Compare here the church of St Anne in Jerusalem (before 1150, left) and the Sultanhanı north of Kayseri of 1232 (right). The pendentives carrying the dome on pointed arches are of identical design. We know that in Frankish Jerusalem the Armenians were highly esteemed as builders, and that the same was true in Fatimid Egypt. In 1074, under Badr Gamali, Armenians built the city walls of Cairo.

commissioned work from these native professionals, artists who had already proved their worth.

Proof of this is to be found in an inscription on a caravanserai near Malatya, the Hekimhanı. There we read: "In the year 667 of the Armenian era, I built this inn." The architect who set down these words was Abu Salim ibn Abul Hasan, who states that he is Syrian and practised medicine. But he wrote these words in Armenian and specified the date in terms of the Armenian calendar, which begins in 551.

What should be concluded from the similarity between Cistercian churches and Selçuk caravanserais? First, that it was Armeno-Syrian builders, heading teams of craftsmen, who worked in Anatolia on the sultans' commissions. And secondly that some of these Armenians, who fled their country in the aftermath of the Battle of Manzikert of 1071, sought refuge in the West. There they introduced the four-centred arch and the pointed vault which came to define Cistercian architecture after they first appeared in Cluny III.

In northern Syria and Armenia, an architectural tradition had been preserved based on the bold church architecture of the first centuries of the Christian era. The distinguishing mark of these builders was their use of pointed vaults and four-centred arches, which appear in the valleys of the Caucasus in the ninth and tenth centuries. The existence of a single tradition in twelfth century Europe and thirteenth century Anatolia is the only possible explanation for the similarities on which we have remarked. A century apart, the same tradition influenced two very different architectural developments in very different parts of the world.

When the sultans' commissions arrived, requiring the building of representative monuments, and, in particular, at the outset of the thirteenth century, the rapid construction of a chain of caravanserais intended as staging posts along the trade routes of Asia Minor, the native architects of east Anatolia responded by building symbolic constructions, using the only spatial vocabulary they knew, that of the Christian church. They therefore adapted their own language to the requirements of their patrons.

Only by this hypothesis can we explain how lofty naves – ill-suited to winter weather – came to form a central element in the building of the Selçuk caravanserais. But this fact in itself provides a key to many aspects of the religious architecture that came into existence under the sultans of Turkish Anatolia.

EARLY OTTOMAN ARCHITECTURE

Developing New Forms

Page 77

The dawn of Ottoman ornament
From its earliest manifestations during the Turkoman Emirates, the art that accompanied the rise of the Ottomans exhibited a Persian influence, and in particular that of the Timurids, with their ornamental floral repertory. From this point forms grew less angular, and the Selçuk style underwent a complete renewal. This treatment of carnations in the relief from the İlyas Bey Camii at Balat (1404), near the ancient city of Miletus, was to establish itself as a convention of Ottoman classicism.

Geometrical inspiration
In parallel with the softening of forms came a proliferation of tiles of different shapes: hexagons, octagons, dodecagons, and so on. Subtle plays of colour were now possible. Both developments are exploited in this panel from the Muradiye at Bursa, which dates from 1426. The panel is based on triangles, squares and hexagons and mixes white, blue and black.

Following the victory of the Mongols at the Kösedağ in 1243, there was turmoil throughout Anatolia. The Rum Sultanate crumbled before the invasion. The Mongols eventually put Keykubad III to death in 1308. In Anatolia, revolts, uprisings and conflicts followed without interruption as the various tribal chiefs attempted to impose their authority on a region from which all authority had departed. The late thirteenth century was the time of the Turkoman Emirates.

Despite the breakdown of authority, the local architectural tradition lost nothing of its vigour. Many *madrasas* were constructed in pure Selçuk style under the Mongol Ilkhan dynasty and under the Karamanids, at Sivas, Erzurum and Niğde.

At the end of the thirteenth century, among the turbulent ethnic groupings whose ambitions were exercised in the north-west of the country were the Ottomans. The advent of Osman I (ruled 1299–1326) saw the beginning of a seemingly inexorable elevation of this tribe and its fortunes. In 1326, after Bursa (ancient Prusa) had been taken, the Osmanlı tribe established their capital there, on the Asiatic coast of the Sea of Marmara; the city stood on the shore opposite its adversary, Constantinople.

During the fourteenth century, profound changes took place whose eventual result was the rapid expansion of the Ottoman domains at the expense of the Byzantine Empire in Europe. In 1361, the town of Adrianopolis (or Adrianople) fell to the Ottomans. Renamed Edirne, it became the sultan's new capital in 1365. Thereafter, the territory of Byzantium began to shrink even further. Constantinople was under threat from all sides; the Turkish forces undertook siege after siege in their attempts to storm the ancient capital of the *basileis*. Byzantium had been besieged by the Arabs in 674–678, and again in 718. The capital was taken by the Crusaders in 1204. When Bulgaria fell to Bayezit I in 1389, Byzantium was again attacked. After routing the Crusaders at Nicopolis in 1396, Bayezit I was free to concentrate his forces against Constantinople, which he did for the next seven years. The Byzantines were saved only by the unexpected arrival in Anatolia of Mongol invaders under Tamerlane (Timur).

The defeat of Sultan Bayezit I by the forces of Tamerlane at Ankara in 1402 was a catastrophe, which came close to destroying the recently established Osmanlı state altogether. Bayezit died in captivity. But in 1405, before he could establish his power, Tamerlane himself died, and after his death his empire fell into disorder.

Ottoman affairs were in chaos, and Tamerlane's death was the signal for a ferocious battle for power. From it, ten years later, emerged the Sultan Mehmet I (1413–1421). To him it fell to restore Turkish influence in Asia Minor. From this point on, the steady ascent of the Ottomans began; the one factor that seemed likely to halt them had been overcome. Let us briefly consider their phenomenal rise.

Murat II (1421–1444 and 1446–1451) undertook a further siege of Constantinople in 1422, but this attempt failed. In Serbia he was more successful. In 1448, at Kosovo, he won a victory that opened up the whole of the Balkans to his armies.

Vienna•

Ofen•

HUNGA

Cluny•

Szege•

Mohács•

FRANCE

Milan•

Genoa•

Venice•

CROATIA

E•

BOSNIA

Florence•

SERBIA

PORTUGAL

Todi•

Ragusa (Dubrovnik)•

Kos•

Rome•

ITALY

MONTENE

SPAIN

Granada•

MEDITERRANEAN SEA

ALBANIA

MACED

CORFU•

EPIRUS

•Préveza

Algiers•

•Lepa

ALGERIA

Mo•

MAGHREB

TUNISIA

Tunis•

SICILY

MALTA

MEDITERRANEAN SEA

TRIPOLITANIA

CYRENAICA

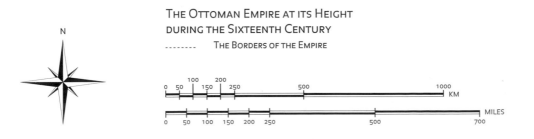

THE OTTOMAN EMPIRE AT ITS HEIGHT
DURING THE SIXTEENTH CENTURY

- - - - - - - -   THE BORDERS OF THE EMPIRE

N

0   50   100   150   200   250   500   1000
                                                              KM

0   50   100 150 200 250   500   700
                                                         MILES

SYLVANIA

BESSARABIA

WALLACHIA

Danube

• Nicopolis

BULGARIA

MELIA

Thrace

Edirne •

Istanbul

Üsküdar

Sea of Marmara

İzmit

İznik

• Bursa

EGEAN
Sea

Lemnos

Chios

• Manisa

Samos

Rhodes

RETE

MEDITERRANEAN SEA

Crimea

Caffa (Feodosiya)

Sea
of Azov

Black Sea

Georgia

Amasya
•

Trebizond
(Trabzon)

Kösedağ

Sivas

Divriği

Erzurum
•

Anatolia

Afyon

Myriocephalon

Konya
•

• Beyşehir

Kayseri

• Aksaray

Niğde

Cappadocia

Binbir Kilise

Cilicia

Cyprus

• İskenderun

• Aleppo (Halab)

Dunaysir
(Kızıltepe)

Diyarbakır

Silvan

Mesopotamia

Dicle (Tigris)

Manzikert
(Malazgirt)

Armenia

• Van

Çaldıran

Tabriz (Tauris)
•

Caspian Sea

Azerbaijan

Gorgan

Persia

Isfahan
•

Syria

Damascus
•

Firat (Euphrates)

• Baghdad

• Jerusalem

Persian Gulf

Egypt

• Cairo

Nile

Al Hijaz

Arabian Peninsula

Medina
•

Red Sea

Mecca
•

Mehmet II succeeded to the Sultanate in 1451, and made the conquest of Constantinople his goal. By now, the former eastern capital of the Roman Empire held only a tiny area outside its walls, and its possessions had been reduced to outposts on the Black Sea and in the Greek islands. In 1453, after a brief siege, the city capitulated. Under the name Istanbul, it became the capital of Mehmet II, and gained for him the title of Fatih, the Conqueror.

The Evolution of the Mosque

These events strongly influenced the course of architecture. In south-west Anatolia, a new tendency in architecture had been evident for close to a century. A style of mosque developed whose prototype was built in 1155: the Ulu Camii (Great Mosque) in Silvan. The layout comprised a partly porticoed courtyard leading to an oblong prayer-hall with a central dome.

An example of this new format is the Ulu Camii or Great Mosque of Manisa, in western Asia Minor, built in 1366. It has four bays of ribbed vaults, forming nineteen squares around the central dome, which itself covers nine. In the Fatih İbrahim Bey Camii at Urla, near Izmir, the prayer-hall is again wider than it is deep. The same tendency is manifest in the south of the country, exemplified in the Lal Ağa Camii at Mut. And it reached the east in 1371, when the Latifiye Camii was built at Mardin; this was followed by the Bab üs-Sur Camii, built in the same town during the second half of the fourteenth century.

The forms of these mosques remain relatively traditional, since they are inspired by the classical Arab oblong plan, to which they add a vast central dome. At the outset of the Ottoman era, this formula was somewhat neglected, though it influenced the Üç Şerefeli Camii at Edirne (begun 1437).

A mature architecture
At Balat, in the Mantese Emirate, stands the İlyas Bey Camii, which dates from 1404. The mosque's harmonious forms illustrate the progress accomplished by Ottoman architecture; its plan, of great clarity, and its coherent volumes are the product of a deliberate classicism. The sober hemispherical dome on its octagonal base and the great arch over the three bays of the portal are further evidence of maturity.

The Ulu Camii

The Great Mosque at Manisa was built in 1366 under the rule of Işak Bey of the Saruhan dynasty. The courtyard porticoes make use of classical columns, which carry raised arches; the tie-beams add to the sense of structural coherence.

Modular organisation

The Ulu Camii is based on a carefully structured, unified plan. The courtyard and prayer-hall cover an identical space, subdivided into twenty-eight units (four by seven). The surface area of the light-well corresponds to that of the dome-baldachin that precedes the *mihrab*. This great dome dominating an oblong room on a horizontal axis is the first example in Ottoman architecture of this format, which recurs in the Üç Şerefeli Camii in Edirne and elsewhere.

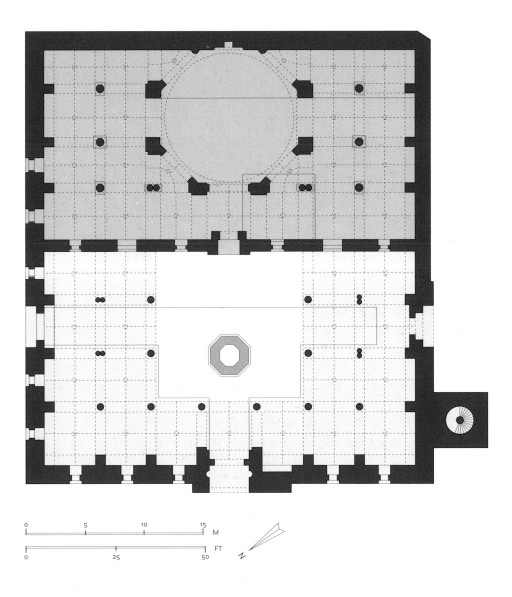

A modest domed building
The Yeşil Camii or Green Mosque in İznik, a very simple building, dates from 1378. The mosque owes its name to the delicately coloured tiles that decorate the body of the minaret, whose galleries are supported by stalactite corbels.

However, in the Mentese Emirate, another type of mosque was gaining currency. This was the single-domed sanctuary, in which the dome covered the entire internal space. The İlyas Bey Camii (1404) in Balat, near the ancient site of Miletus, is a fine example of this plan. It is a rigorous and highly unified building, whose square prayer-hall, without a portal, is crowned by an octagonal drum supporting the dome. This was very early for a building of this design, and is worthy of note, as its style is more progressive than that of Ottoman architecture of the same period. The purity of its elevation, the clarity of its ornamentation, which is confined to the door and the lattice work on either side of it, and the elegance of the great pointed arch that rises over the porch, established it as a model of its kind, despite a certain solidity which means that the interior has insufficient natural light. This characteristic of Ottoman architecture was to remain noticeable until the first works of the architect Hayrettin under Bayezit II.

The Originality of the Ottomans at İznik and Bursa

The first buildings in a truly original Ottoman style were built in İznik and Bursa. The Yeşil Camii or Green Mosque in İznik (Byzantine Nicaea) dates from 1378. In Bursa (ancient Prusa), a whole series of monuments were constructed between 1391 and 1451 by the Sultans Murat I, Yıldırım Bayezit, Mehmet I, and Murat II.

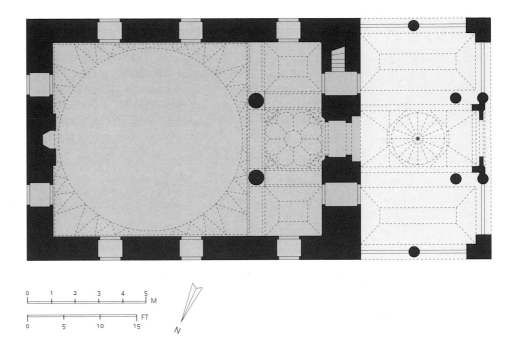

A sober plan
The Yeşil Camii in İznik has a rectangular prayer-hall preceded by a porch. The dome is connected to the square base by Turkish pleats. The three bays of the entrance open on to the prayer-hall.

The Green Mosque of İznik owes its name to its solitary brick minaret; the lower part, and its top gallery, supported on stalactite vaults, have a revetment of blue-green tiles. The building is entered through a portal, and comprises a small square prayer-hall capped by a hemispherical dome on a drum. The marble of which it is built probably came from classical sites.

The focus of attention in this building is the portico with its two sets of three arcades. The slightly pointed arches are set on reused classical columns; between them are fine lattice-work panels with star motifs. At the base of the capitals, which exhibit a highly stylised foliage design, there is a row of *muqarnas*. The heavy framework of the portal is flanked by a stalactite frieze. This ornamental vocabulary is all but identical with that of the Selçuks. But the building as a whole is quite distinctive; its restricted internal space and its strict and compact character are quite unlike the Selçuk mosques.

The tile revetment of the minaret is a reminder that from the fifteenth to the eighteenth centuries İznik was a great centre for the production of glazed polychrome tiles. The artists of Tabriz, brought to İznik in the aftermath of the wars between Turkey and Persia, developed the art of ornamental ceramics in the Ottoman domains, thus propagating a tradition that had originated in Mongol and Timurid Persia.

Before turning to the Ottoman tradition proper, one building must be mentioned: the Great Mosque or Ulu Camii in Bursa, built in 1396. It is a fine hypostyle hall of five naves and four bays, on whose twelve square pillars sit twenty little domes. This traditional plan was replaced in the Ottoman world by the charitable foundations endowed by the sultans.

For Ottoman art was in search of new architectural solutions. In Bursa, for the first time, there appear prayer-halls with a very individual plan, in which two domes are aligned. The two main domes, set one behind the other, are the distinguishing feature of a form of mosque that prevailed in the Ottoman world until the capture of Constantinople in 1453. Characteristic examples are the Murat Paşa Camii in Istanbul, built in 1466, and the mosque of Bayezit II at Amasya, which dates from 1486.

In Bursa, the main building of this kind is the Yıldırım Bayezit Camii, built between 1389 and 1402 by the Sultan Bayezit I. It forms part of a *külliye* comprising

the mosque, a *madrasa*, the *türbe* of the founder, a *hammam*, and various kiosks. The mosque itself has an imposing porch, with five small domes and *muqarna* decoration. However, the junction between the two domed areas of the interior is rather awkwardly handled.

In buildings of this kind, the first dome is flanked by two smaller domes, which buttress it. The second domed space contains the *mihrab*, which forms a kind of projecting chevet. The result is the inverted "T"-shape characteristic of the earliest Ottoman mosques. The oblong format of Arab prayer-halls has been replaced by a longitudinal space on the model of Christian churches, and the broadening of the building where the lateral domes extend it is analogous to a transept.

The architectural use of ceramics, which we have quoted at İznik, is also found at Bursa, in the Yeşil Camii and the Yeşil Türbe (the word *yeşil* means "green"). The Yeşil Camii was built in 1419 and the *türbe* for Mehmet I in 1421 by an architect named Haçı İvaz; he was assisted in the ceramic ornamentation by one Ali from Tabriz. Here again, the mosque comprises two domes set one behind the other. The two domes (the biggest is only 12.5 m in diameter) rest on a dome with "Turkish pleats". This is a solution to the problem of placing a circular dome on a square base, and uses only rectilinear geometrical forms, in order to avoid pendentives of spherical section. The result is an intermediate zone animated by the reflections of the angular pleats between the calm surfaces of the prayer-hall walls and the *intrados* of the dome.

Just as the Byzantine church featured an imperial *loggia*, where the *basileus* sat while Mass was celebrated, so the Green Mosque in Bursa contains a sultan's *loge*; it is set above the axial entrance, and is entirely covered with an astonishing revetment of green tiles with golden overtones. It formed a sort of jewel case in which the sultan was enclosed. From this point on, polychrome ceramic decoration was no

An awkward solution
The three bays of the entrance portico of the Yeşil Camii in İznik have pointed arches; the central arch is higher and wider. On either side, the balustrades with their marble *claustra* display a handsome geometry. The entrance is framed by stalactites carved in strong relief. The overall organisation remains somewhat clumsy; the juxtaposition of the framed doorway and the columns (reused classical examples) ultimately fails to convince.

Rows of *muqarnas*
The portal leading into the Ulu Camii (Great Mosque) at Bursa is decorated with a handsome masonry stalactite vault forming a semi-dome.

Tradition and innovation
The Ulu Camii at Bursa dates from 1396. In the hypostyle prayer-hall, square pillars with large pointed arches carry the domes. Its central light-well is in accordance with Selçuk tradition, but its rows of domes foreshadow the new Otto-man styles.

Left
A two-domed hall
A view of the two different domes of the Yıldırım Bayezit Camii in Bursa. The internal space beneath them is basilican in format. Early Ottoman architecture mostly did not adopt the oblong shape traditional in Arab prayer-halls.

Right
The quest for a formula
The unusual silhouette of the Yıldırım Bayezit Camii, built between 1389 and 1402, shows a minaret flanking the vestibule and two domes of unequal size. The use of rows of domes derives from the Byzantine tradition.

The discovery of a formula
The entrance portico is roofed with five domes. The rhythms imparted by the repetition of the square module are enhanced by the depressed arches. Porches of this design evolved as a transition between internal and external spaces, and are equally characteristic of Byzantine architecture.

Page 89
Complex articulation
The internal organisation of the Yıldırım Bayezit mosque at Bursa is dominated by the two domes. The "side-aisles" roofed with small domes determine the T-shaped plan. To the left, the sanctuary comprising the *mihrab* (only the *minbar* is visible here) is slightly raised, as are the "side-aisles". A large basket arch marks the division between the two internal spaces; access to the "side-aisles" is via pointed arches.

Left

Mosaic decoration

The Yeşil ("Green") Türbe in Bursa was built by Mehmet I in 1421. The use of polychrome ceramic decoration is an indication of Timurid influence. On either side of the entrance portal are stalactite niches, richly ornamented with glazed brick, in which floral motifs alternate with inscriptions.

Above right

An octagonal mausoleum

The Yeşil Türbe is a tower-mausoleum in the Selçuk tradition. It is octagonal in plan, with a projecting portal.

Below right

Turkish pleats

The architect makes use of Turkish pleats at the corners of the entrance portal. This device, original to Turkey, enables the transition from right angle to circle and eliminates the need for pendentives and squinches. Here the pleats are seen above a stalactite frieze.

Page 91

The splendour of the imperial *loge*

Byzantine churches had *loggie* for the *basileus* (emperor); Ottoman sultanic mosques had sumptuous *loges* for the sultan. Construction of the Yeşil Camii (Green Mosque) at Bursa started in 1419. It was built for Mehmet I and contains a *loge* entirely covered in tiles and gold mosaic-work. A curious stalactite frieze marks the junction of walls and ceiling.

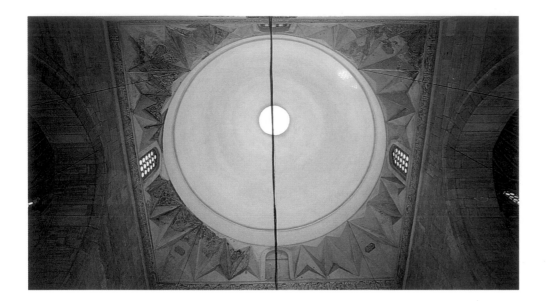

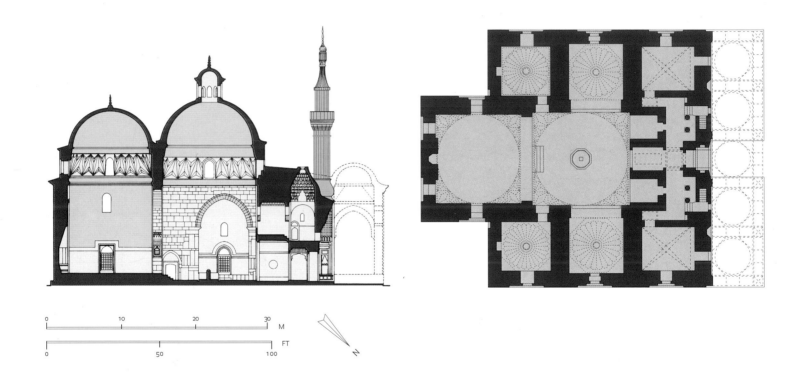

longer confined to the exterior of buildings; it covered the entire internal space and even the slender stalactites at the junction between walls and ceiling. A very slight relief element emphasises the lattice of star and octagon motifs that predominate in this sumptuous decoration.

The entrance was at one time preceded by a porch set on columns with five small domes. Like the Yıldırım Bayezit Camii, the Green Mosque of Bursa has no court-yard. But, in combination with the other buildings, it forms a *külliye*, or religious complex; there is a *madrasa* and a *türbe* in addition to the mosque, and all these form part of the same foundation. The *türbe* is the Yeşil Türbe of Bursa, the mausoleum of Mehmet I. Octagonal in form, it follows the traditional plan of Selçuk funer-ary monuments. Its portal is surmounted by a ribbed niche, and is decorated with stalactites and Turkish pleats, enhanced by ceramic mosaics in the style of the Timurid works of Persia.

The plan of two successive domes is also found in the Muradiye, the mosque of the *külliye* of Murat I, dating from 1426. This formula obviously derives from

A rigorous design

The chevet of the Murat Paşa Camii, built at Bursa in 1426. Here the quest for a formula has produced a building of great volumetric coherence and strict symmetry. The prayer-hall is cubic, the hemispherical dome sits on an octagonal drum, and the composition is framed by two minarets.

Inside the Muradiye

A view across the mosque of Murat Paşa, from one side-aisle to the other. A very individual space is created by the two aligned domes, the depressed arches and the partly raised floor. The curious pendentives are covered in *muqarnas* and star motifs.

A polychrome ceiling
The polychrome coffered ceiling combines with the geometrical polychrome tiles in the porch of the Muradiye in Bursa. The array of hexagonal motifs is interrupted by stalactite mouldings in the corners.

Ottoman tombs
Some of the tomb buildings around the Muradiye at Bursa are square, some octagonal; all are roofed with a dome set on a drum. To the left, the Murat II complex; to the right, the mausoleum of Prince Ahmet.

Page 95
An ambulatory around the tomb
Internal view of the tomb of Murat II, built in 1451. The cenotaph of the sultan lies under the dome, which is supported by columns and corner pillars. The octagonal drum is made possible by small stalactite squinches. The ambulatory facilitated the practice of ritual circumambulation.

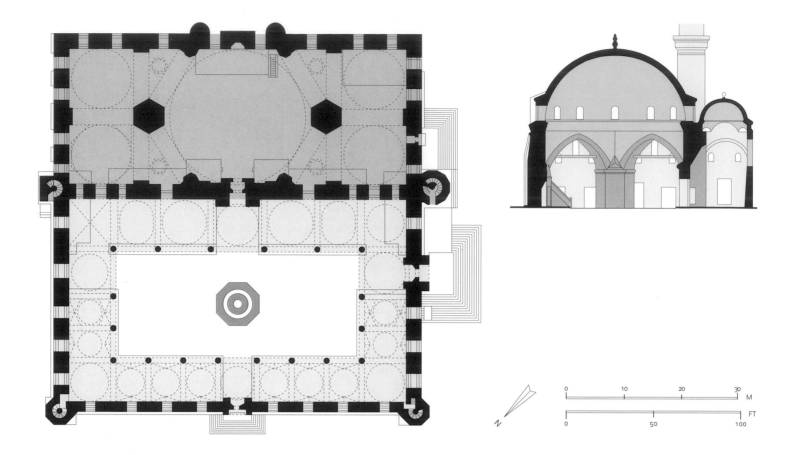

Byzantine buildings (St Irene of Constantinople, which in turn derives from St John of Ephesus), and marks a turning point in the development of Islamic architecture. The longitudinal emphasis is attenuated because the floor of the space under the second dome is raised, but it remains evident, while the openings that join the "nave" to the "side-aisles" do nothing to counterpoise this emphasis.

The decoration of the Muradiye includes pleats at the base of the dome, and pendentives whose joints are covered in stalactites. There are numerous mosaic plinths in polychrome ceramics, in which blue, black and white are the predominant colours.

In the Bursa *külliye*, Murat II also built a series of *türbes*, one of which was to be his own mausoleum and was built in 1451. The plan that he chose for this facilitated ritual circumambulation; an ambulatory surrounds the alternating pillars and columns that support the dome.

A Reaction: The Üç Şerefeli at Edirne

Eleven years after the mosque he built in Bursa, Murat II commissioned the Üç Şerefeli Camii which was constructed in Edirne between 1437 and 1447. This is a large mosque on a very different model from the two-domed style. It seems to mark a return to the style of buildings such as those at Mut, Mardin and Manisa that were described earlier in the chapter.

This huge mosque covers a space 65 by 67 m (4 200 m²) and presents an oblong prayer-hall (transverse *haram*) covered with a large dome, 24 m in diameter, on a hexagonal base. The central dome rests on two enormous piers, and is buttressed by a pair of smaller domes 11 m in diameter. A porticoed courtyard runs the full length of the prayer-hall.

This was a highly ambitious undertaking, as its scale suggests: indeed, something of a gamble. Though the central dome is lit by twelve bays, the space within remains dark. And the prayer-hall is not very high relative to its massive structure –

An original design
In Edirne, north-west of Istanbul, the Üç Şerefeli Camii was constructed by Murat II in 1437–1447. The general plan and section of the prayer-hall show it to be a veritable architectural laboratory. The porticoes forming the oblong courtyard have heterogeneous vaults: domes of various diameters, intersecting ribs, and oval domes. On the entrance side, the courtyard has eight columns; on the prayer-hall side, six. The hall itself is oblong, and comprises a huge central hexagonal dome with two smaller domes on either side. The great internal arches spring from powerful hexagonal piers.

A complex unity

A view of the roof of the Üç Şerefeli Camii in Edirne clearly shows the roofing method. To the right is the great dome, and to the left, one of the umbrella vaults. Between them a triangular structure is created by the restraining arches, which spring from hexagonal piers.

Interior of the Üç Şerefeli

Within the Üç Şerefeli Camii, the space created by the 25-m diameter of the great dome is revealed as dark and oppressive. Before Hayrettin and Sinan, it seemed impossible to create a lofty space beneath a single dome.

Under a spiral-ornamented minaret
Though its domes and vaults are not uniform, the courtyard of the Üç Şerefeli Camii in Edirne is the most successful element of this experimental building. It displays all the characteristics of the best Ottoman architecture, being light, airy and graceful.

A descendant of the Byzantine atrium
The alternating red and white voussoirs and exceptionally slender monolithic columns impart a graceful rhythm to the courtyard of the Üç Şerefeli Camii. Little domes on their drums are visible above the portico.

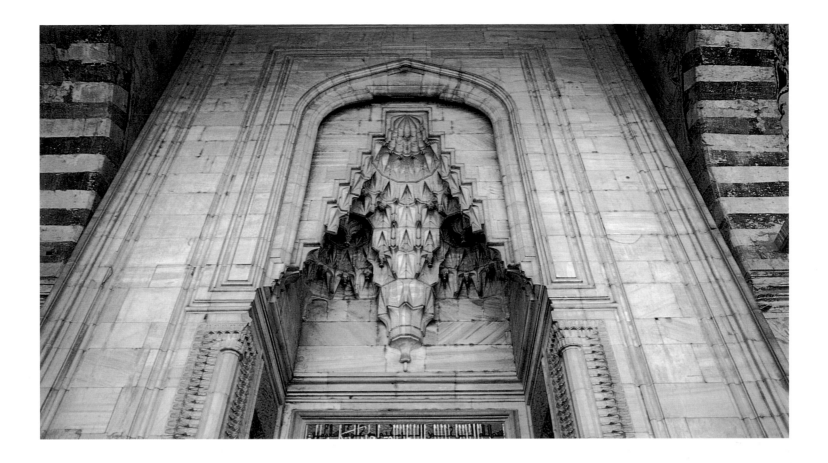

Emergence of classical Ottoman ornament
The stalactite niche above the door to the prayer-hall in the Üç Şerefeli Camii in Edirne. In its combination of deeply carved elements let into patterned flat surfaces, it displays the full maturity of Ottoman art.

the keystone is at 28 m – so that the overall effect is heavy and cramped. There is little mastery of load-bearing techniques, and those employed are often spatially intrusive. The buttressing triangles that flank the hexagon, with their thick arches, are particularly eloquent proof of this. And the segmental profile of the dome contributes to the slightly oppressive effect.

By contrast, the portico that constitutes the inner façade of the courtyard, with its central şadırvan, already exhibits the graceful proportions of "classic" Ottoman architecture. Its design nevertheless shows evidence of naivety: the domes are of differing diameters, and some are oval in order to compensate for the irregularities caused by the presence of the doors. There are nine small domes on the side of the main entrance, as against seven irregular domes on the prayer-hall side. In short, the Üç Şerefeli Camii at Edirne is a major step forward, but cannot be accounted a complete success.

Bayezit II and his Architect Hayrettin

The Sultan Bayezit II (1481–1512), who inherited the throne of Mehmet II the Conqueror, left two major buildings that have ensured that his name comes down to posterity: the Edirne *külliye* and his sultanic mosque in Istanbul. Thanks to the strong personality of his architect Hayrettin – the presumed author of these works – Ottoman art attained its maturity under his reign, though the finest masterpieces of Ottoman architecture came somewhat later, with the works of Sinan the Great.

Like his father, Bayezit II was strongly interested in the West; in 1501, he asked Leonardo da Vinci to construct a bridge on the Golden Horn. The project never went beyond sketches and plans. Around 1504, the same proposition was put to Michelangelo. His travelling expenses were to be paid by the sultan via the Gondi Bank in Florence, but Pope Julius II refused to countenance his departure.

The work of Bayezit II at Edirne is a huge complex begun in 1484 and finished by 1488. In one vast *külliye* were set two *madrasas*, a mosque with porticoed courtyard,

A Grandiose Design: the Fatih *külliye* at Istanbul

A dominant citadel
The Ottomans built powerful fortresses on the straits to reinforce the siege of Byzantium. The citadel of Rumeli Hisari, built by Mehmet II in 1452 (a year before the city was captured) stands at the narrowest point of the Bosphorus.

The capture of Constantinople by Mehmet II the Conqueror (1451–1481) was a profound stimulus to Ottoman architecture. Aspirations were enhanced by daily contact with the masterpieces of Byzantium and the sense that the Ottomans had inherited Byzantium's imperial prestige. There followed a demand for new and symbolic monuments, to be built on a scale commensurate with the size of the Ottoman empire. Istanbul was to receive a series of great buildings comparable with the masterpieces of Christian Byzantium.

Mehmet II surrounded himself with scholars, artists and technicians from Greece, Italy and Central Europe. The sultan aspired to know and understand the latest developments in the arts and sciences. He was the first Muslim to take an interest in artillery and he entrusted the production of his cannons to German metalsmiths. Mehmet Fatih was only twenty-four years old when he captured Byzantium, and sought a "modernity" compatible with his years. His lucidity was exemplary. He was anything but a fanatic, and took a considerable interest in Christianity, which was the faith of his mother. He protected the Jews, and studied the tenets of the Persian Shiite school. He had the works of Latin and Greek authors read to him, notably those of Seneca, Polybius, and Claudius Ptolemy. He appreciated Western art, and, late in his life, invited the painter Gentile Bellini to his court.

It was in this spirit that he decided to construct a sultanic mosque in Istanbul. The foundations of the mosque and its immense *külliye* were laid on the ruins of the Church of the Holy Apostles, constructed by Justinian on one of the hills of Constantinople. The church had been in ruins since the Frankish depredations of the Fourth Crusade (1199–1204). The architect whom he chose was a Christian, Christodoulos, better known under his Turkish name of Atik Sinan (Sinan the Elder), which distinguishes him from the great Sinan who later worked for Süleyman and Selim II. The architect broke completely with the Bursa school.

The Fatih Camii (Mosque of the Conqueror) was built between 1463 and 1471, at the centre of a *külliye* occupying an area 320 m square. It was destroyed by an earthquake in 1766. The mosque that replaced it was built in 1767 on an entirely different plan, drawing its inspiration in equal part from the Şehzade of Sinan and the Blue Mosque of Mehmet Ağa. But we know from excavations and contemporary engravings that the Mosque of the Conqueror showed the influence of Haghia Sophia: it had an oblong, porticoed courtyard set around the *şadırvan*, and was of imposing size: 96 by 56 m.

The prayer-hall was covered with a dome 26 m in diameter, and there was a further, rectangular space covered with a semi-dome above the *mihrab*. On either side of the central dome, a range of three small domes buttressed the ensemble. We see in this formula a smaller-scale version of the central and rear part of Justinian's Byzantine basilica. The front part, with its semi-dome, was eliminated; this alteration probably reflected the requirement for an oblong prayer hall of the kind traditional in classical Islam. But it may also have contributed to the collapse of the building, since it deprived it of buttressing on its north façade.

The remaining buildings of the Fatih *külliye* have survived and allow us to grasp the scale of the complex. Unlike the religious foundations at Bursa, which were widely scattered in rather haphazard fashion, the Fatih complex has a strictly rectilinear organisation. There are eight *madrasas*, each with a courtyard whose inner façade is porticoed, eight buildings set lengthways along the sides of the complex (these were shops and accommodation), an *imaret* or people's refectory, a caravanserai and *türbes* (mausolea). The rigorously symmetrical disposition of the complex is still visible on its esplanade, which commands excellent views of the city.

This magnificently designed ensemble was on a much larger scale than most Renaissance building programmes in the West; it was also much more functional. The combination of scale and function made the Fatih *külliye* a paradigm for future Ottoman architecture.

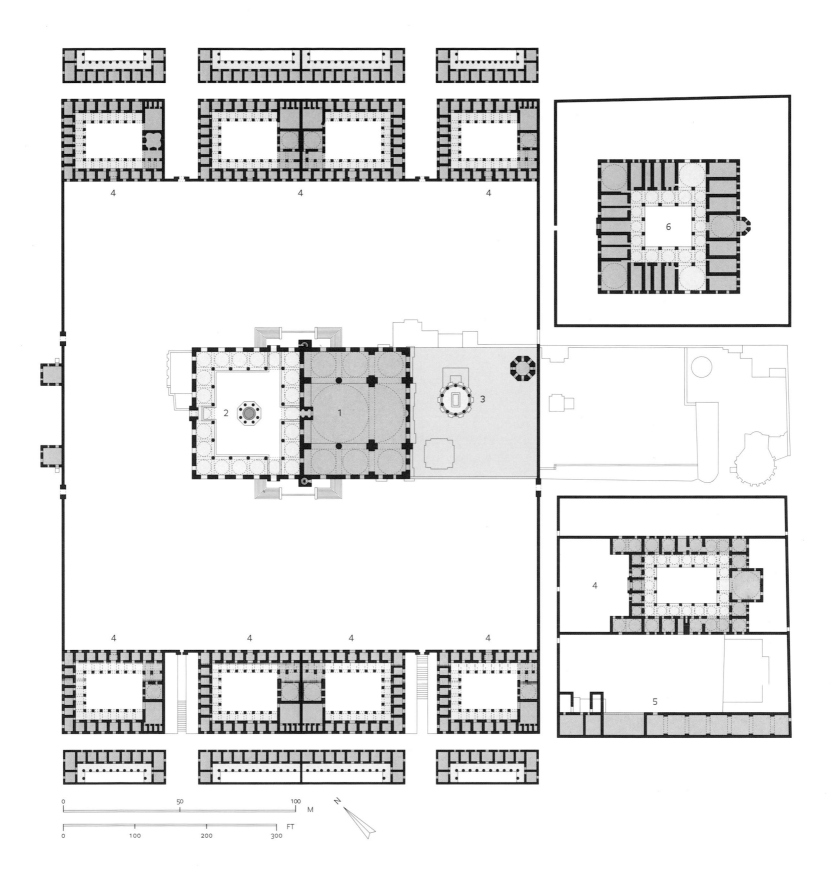

In commemoration of victory

In 1453, Mehmet II Fatih (the Conqueror) conquered Constantinople, which thereupon became Istanbul. On the site of the ruined Byzantine church of the Holy Apostles he built a mosque surrounded by a group of public buildings: *madrasa*, library, *imaret* (popular refectory), caravanserais and *türbe*. This immense complex, a *külliye* or charitable foundation, was built between 1463 and 1471. The Fatih Camii stands at the centre of the complex, which covers ten hectares. Its symmetrical layout and huge open spaces are the work of the architect Atik Sinan (Sinan the Elder, as distinct from the more famous Sinan who worked for Süleyman and Selim II).

1 Mosque
2 Courtyard
3 *Türbe*
4 *Madrasa*
5 Caravanserai
6 Library

An outstanding success

The huge *külliye* built in
1484–1488 by Sultan Bayezit II
(1481–1512) in Edirne may legit-
imately be described as the first
masterpiece of Ottoman art.
Designed by the architect Hayrettin, the complex includes a
mosque, a hospital, a mental asylum, a school of medicine, a popular
refectory, a bakery and a pair of
madrasas. The design plays on contrasts, on the soaring verticality
of the minarets and the formulas
repeated throughout the complex
such as the rows of domes flanked
by chimneys, and perfectly combines rigour of conception with
an element of the picturesque.

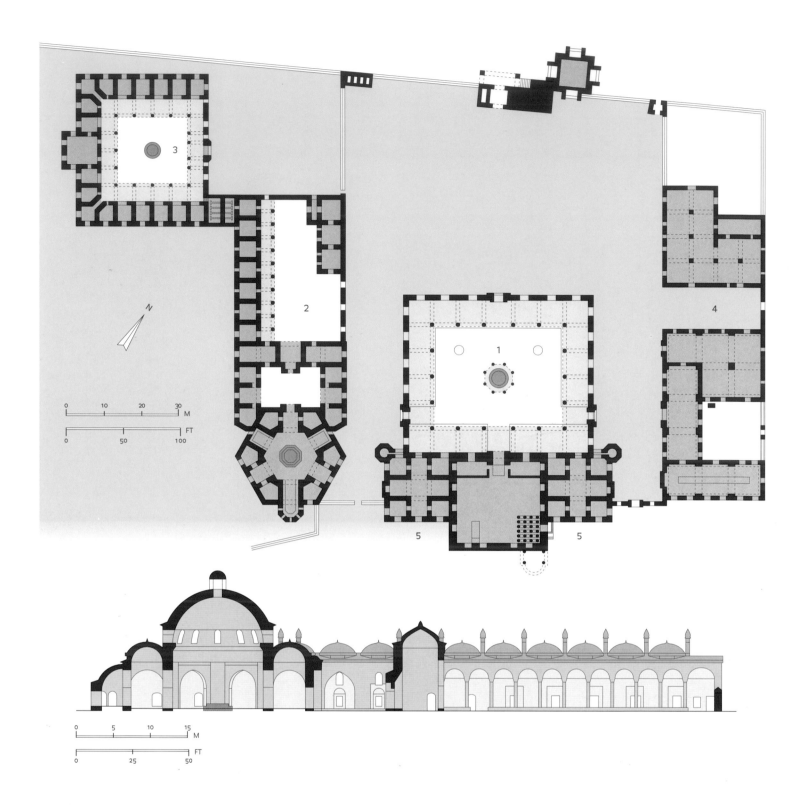

Clarity of design

A view across the courtyard of the mosque in the *külliye* of Bayezit II at Edirne. The placing of a column on the axis is characteristic of the work of the architect Hayrettin in both Edirne and Istanbul.

Page 104 above
The *külliye* of Bayezit II
Constructed in the late fifteenth century, the buildings of the complex bring together material and spiritual concerns.
1 Mosque
2 Hospital and mental asylum
3 School of medicine
4 Popular refectory and bakery
5 *Madrasa* and library

Below: longitudinal section of the mental asylum, in which hydrotherapy and treatment by music were practised. The relative lack of symmetry of the Bayezit complex contrasts with the strict organisation of the Fatih *külliye* in Istanbul.

Majesty and sobriety
Axial view of the courtyard of the Bayezit II mosque at Edirne. The dome sits on a cubic base, flanked by two minarets, which emphasise the perfect symmetry of the building. The broad arcades carrying the little domes of the portico rest on contrastingly slender monolithic columns.

a school of medicine, an asylum for the insane, a hospital and an *imaret* or people's refectory. The entire complex is aligned around the mosque, which is cube-shaped in structure and covered with a single dome measuring 23 m in diameter. It is connected to the square plan by smooth pendentives carrying a drum of twenty sides, in which twenty windows are pierced. They illuminate an austere interior. Another fourteen openings in the side wall add to the impression that the building is flooded with light.

The mosque itself is flanked by two square *madrasas*. They have a transverse structure, in which the width of the main hall is equal to the depth of the hall and courtyard. At the front corner of each *madrasa* stands one of the pair of minarets that frame the composition.

But from an aesthetic point of view, the most satisfying element in the complex is the asylum. Its northern section consists of a courtyard with a very graceful asymmetrical portico. Its southern section displays a hexagonal central plan, with a thermal basin placed under the dome and lantern; the main part of the building is 85 m long. This central dome is surrounded by twelve small domes. The extremely pure and austere lines of the asylum are emphasised by the neatly dressed stonework.

The unity of the consecrated space

The prayer-hall of the Bayezit II mosque in Edirne exhibits great spatial unity. The many windows in the walls produce an even illumination. The large pendentives support the base of a single dome, 23 m in diameter, resting on a drum lit by twenty windows. In the centre, the *mihrab*; to its left, the *dikka*; to its right, the *minbar*.

The overall plan of the Bayezit II *külliye* at Edirne is still somewhat irregular. But the very freedom of organisation within certain constraints is part of its fascination. At his first attempt, then, Hayrettin designed a complex of great heterogeneity for his sultan; though it does not possess the rigorous symmetry of the Fatih *külliye* in Istanbul, it is one of the first flowers of Ottoman classicism.

This maturity of style is further confirmed by Hayrettin's design for the sultanic mosque of Bayezit II at Istanbul, constructed on what had been the Forum Tauri of Theodosius. The mosque was begun in 1501 and is clearly inspired by Haghia Sophia, though only half the latter's size. There is a central dome, with a semi-dome at the entrance and chevet. The internal dimensions of the prayer-hall that resulted are 40 by 40 m: 1600 m². These dimensions are in striking contrast with those of Justinian's Haghia Sophia, whose internal space is 5 600 m².

The Bayezit Camii, with its porticoed courtyard, is 84 m long and 42 m wide, and consists of two squares; its lateral extensions, which complete its "T"-shape, are also 84 m in length. The *atrium* and basilica of Haghia Sophia alone occupy a space 140 m long and 74 m wide. In short, the dimensions of the two buildings differ widely. But the Bayezit II mosque makes it clear that the structures of the Byzantine model were deliberately imitated: the dome buttressed by two semi-domes, the

A design of prodigious invention
Based on a hexagonal plan, the
mental asylum was designed to
permit thermal treatment, and
allowed the architect Hayrettin to
demonstrate his mastery of form
and volume. The central dome
with its elegant lantern is surrounded by a series of twelve
smaller domes. The roofing is
lead-sheet over a timber frame.
The roofscape is completed by the
jaunty verticality of the chimneys.

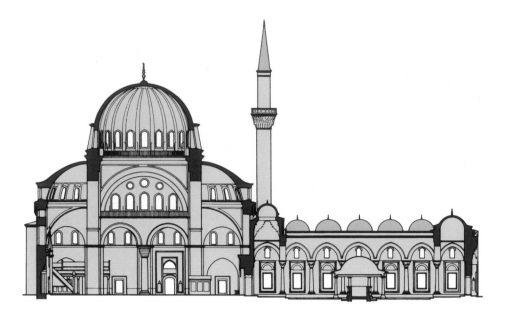

The *şadırvan*

In the centre of the courtyard of the Bayezit Camii in Istanbul stands the ritual fountain, sheltered by a kiosk resting on eight columns, which seem to be classical *spolia*.

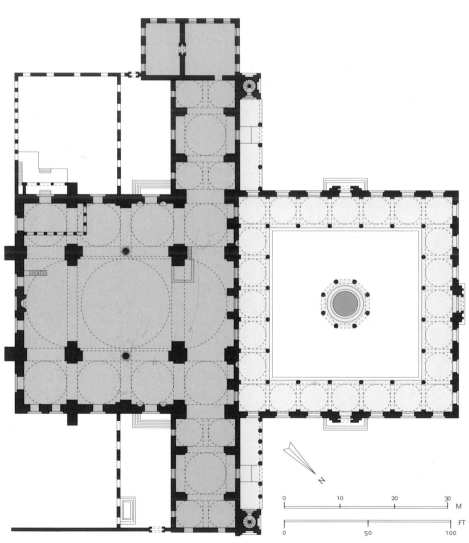

The Bayezit Camii in Istanbul

Longitudinal section and plan of the Bayezit Camii in Istanbul, built by Sultan Bayezit II between 1501 and 1506. The square courtyard (seven by seven domes) exactly matches the area of the prayer-hall. The latter comprises a single central dome buttressed by two semi-domes; the side-aisles each comprise a row of four little domes. Hayrettin's building is clearly inspired by Haghia Sophia, designed a thousand years before by Anthemios of Tralles and Isidorus of Miletus. Hayrettin's references to Haghia Sophia were continued in the work of Sinan.

Arches and domes
Construction of the Bayezit Camii
in Istanbul began in 1501. Centre,
the main dome resting on smooth
pendentives and supported on
either side by tympana. Top left,
one of the pair of buttressing
semi-domes. Top right, one of the
small domes of the side-aisles.
This arrangement was followed
by Sinan in the larger and more
complex Süleymaniye.

longitudinal nave flanked by double arcades, above which are tympana pierced with
numerous windows and connected to the dome by pendentives, the reused classical
columns (one on each side in the mosque, four in Haghia Sophia), and so on. From
this point on, with exceptions, the Byzantine influence tended to prevail.

If we compare the mosque of Bayezit II to the original Fatih Camii, elements of
which the Bayezit mosque also borrows – notably the two great columns on the
sides of the main dome and the system of buttressing – the later mosque is more
coherent and more rigorously geometrical. The overall effect is very satisfying,
though the internal space is not, perhaps, as lofty as one might desire. Equally satisfying is the square, porticoed courtyard flanked by seven domes on each side; its
axial doorways lead directly to the *şadırvan*.

The work of Hayrettin highlights the difficulties that later faced Sinan and Süleyman, as our study of the motives behind the plan adopted for the Süleymaniye Camii
makes clear. But his work also offers a first indication of the developments introduced by the master architect Sinan in his dialogue with the Byzantine tradition,
a dialogue that was to produce a new and original conception of the Turkish mosque.

Süleyman and the Ottoman Golden Age

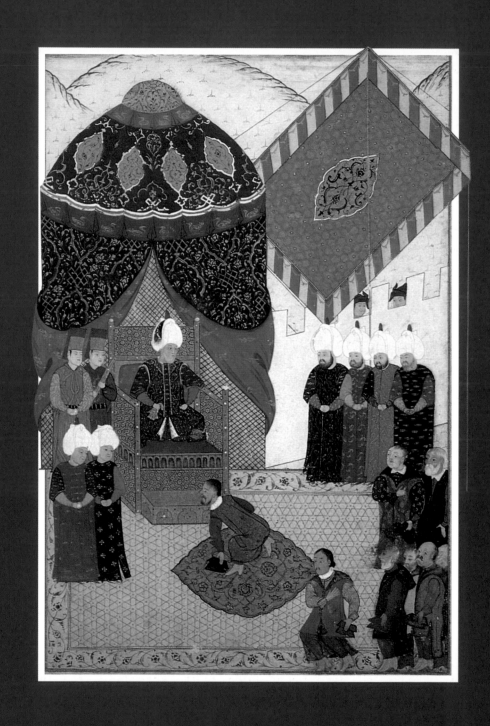

Sinan, Architect to the Sultan

Page 113

Süleyman the Magnificent
This was the title given in the West to the most glorious of the Ottoman sovereigns. Süleyman is portrayed as aquiline, shrewd and dark-bearded in this miniature from the *Şahmail-Name*, painted around 1580 by Osman. (Library of the Topkapı Sarayı Museum, Istanbul)

Court protocol
In his state tent in the Turkish camp at Szigetvar in Hungary, Sultan Süleyman receives John Zápolya, Prince of Transylvania, who bows very low. The Hungarian delegation looks on. This miniature (300 by 200 mm) is from the Chronicle of Ahmed Feridun Paşa, dedicated in 1568–1569 to the Grand Vizier Mehmet Paşa Sokollu. (Library of the Topkapı Sarayı Museum, Istanbul)

The formidable Selim I (1512–1520) defeated the Shah of Persia, annexed Kurdistan, conquered the Mamluks of Cairo, brought Egypt and the Holy Places of Medina and Mecca under Ottoman sway, and, assuming the title of Caliph, made the Ottoman sultans the heads of the Muslim community. Süleyman, his son, was a Renaissance sovereign in every sense. His reign, the longest of the Ottoman dynasty (1520–1566), was one great sequence of victories and heroic feats of arms. In 1521, he captured Belgrade; in 1522, Rhodes surrendered, and its Knights Hospitallers were forced to evacuate the island; in 1526, the Battle of Mohács placed Hungary within the Turkish orbit; in 1534, Tabriz and Baghdad fell; in 1541, central Hungary was annexed; in 1548, the Ottomans wrested the Armenian town of Van from Persian hands.

He was not invincible. In 1529, the Ottomans' fruitless siege of Vienna was lifted. And in 1565, the Turkish fleet failed to storm Malta and again defeat the Knights Hospitallers, despite three months of constant assault from behind the Ottoman blockade. Malta occupied a strategic position in the Mediterranean, and kept the Ottoman Empire from full communication with its possessions on the Algerian coast, which were held by the "Barbary pirate" Khair ed-Din (Turkish Hairettin), better known as Barbarossa.

Süleyman suffered three personal tragedies: the disgrace of his vizier and favourite Ibrahim, a Greek slave of Christian origin who was executed in the palace in 1536; the death at Manisa, in 1543, of his son and heir apparent, Prince Mehmet; and the execution in 1553 of the next heir, another son, Prince Mustafa, who was convicted of treason during the war with Shah Tahmasp of Persia.

Extraordinary Times

The sixteenth century was a time of epoch-making events, whose consequences were felt throughout the world. In 1521, Luther's break with the Pope was officially confirmed by his excommunication. In 1522, the companions of the Portuguese navigator Magellan returned with a single ship from the first global circumnavigation. The world was clearly a finite entity, and the West sought to lay claim to it. In 1521, the Conquistadores of the Emperor Charles V, also king of Spain, overran the Aztec empire; in 1532, the empire of the Incas in its turn fell to Spain. The Holy Roman Emperor now reigned over an empire on which the sun never set. François I, alarmed at this development, offered to ally himself with the Turkish Sultan in order to bring down Charles V; in 1537, the naval battle between Andrea Doria, commander of the Venetian fleet, and the Ottoman corsairs led to the peace of 1540.

It was a time when the influence of Western artists such as Michelangelo (1475–1564), Giulio Romano (1499–1546), Vignola (1507–1573) and Palladio (1508–1580) was felt even in the Ottoman court. In a portal, a row of domes, an arcade or the outline of a building one may suddenly and unexpectedly discern the influence of a Western master.

In artistic terms, the reign of Süleyman was marked by an extraordinary architectural flowering, a series of monuments of imperishable splendour. The out-

standing achievement is the work of Süleyman's court architect, Sinan the Great (1489–1588), who built no less than 355 buildings or complexes: 81 great mosques, 50 prayer-halls, 62 *madrasas*, 19 mausolea or *türbes*, 17 caravanserais, three hospitals, and seven aqueducts. Above all, Sinan built the sultanic mosques of Süleyman at Istanbul and of Süleyman's successor, Selim II, at Edirne. The Selimiye is his masterpiece.

Süleyman was an eminent patron of the arts and an eminent jurist. His legal heritage is among the most important of the Islamic world; he unified the legislation of the Empire. In Islamic lands his title is not Süleyman the Magnificent, but Süleyman the Legislator (*Kanuni*), and his reputation equals that of Justinian, the greatest legislator of the classical world.

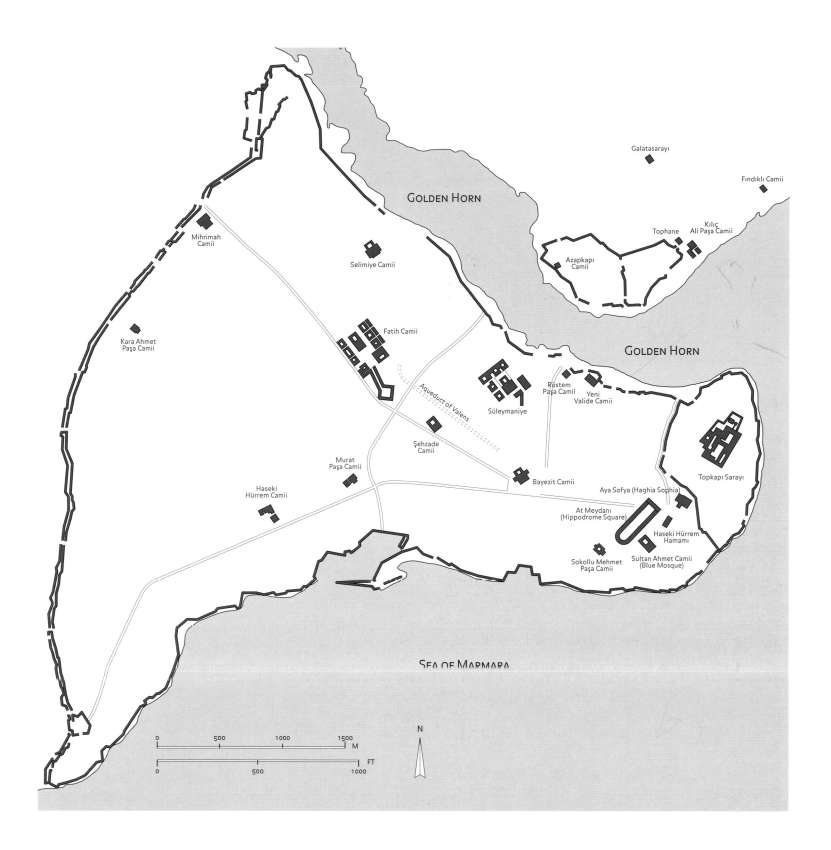

GALATASARAYI

Fındıklı Camii

GOLDEN HORN

Kılıç Ali Paşa Camii

Tophane

Azapkapı Camii

Mihrimah Camii

Selimiye Camii

GOLDEN HORN

Kara Ahmet Paşa Camii

Fatih Camii

Rüstem Paşa Camii

Yeni Valide Camii

Aqueduct of Valens

Süleymaniye

Topkapı Sarayı

Şehzade Camii

Murat Paşa Camii

Bayezit Camii

Haseki Hürrem Camii

Aya Sofya (Haghia Sophia)

At Meydanı (Hippodrome Square)

Haseki Hürrem Hamamı

Sokollu Mehmet Paşa Camii

Sultan Ahmet Camii (Blue Mosque)

SEA OF MARMARA

0   500   1000   1500
M

0   500   1000
FT

N

The fortified city inherited from Justinian
A plan of Istanbul in the sixteenth and seventeenth centuries, showing the sites of the principal Ottoman monuments and the land and sea walls surrounding the Turkish capital.

Sinan's first masterpiece
Plan and longitudinal section of
the Şehzade Camii in Istanbul. It
was built as the sultanic mosque
of Süleyman in 1543 by the architect Sinan. The building comprises
two quadrilaterals of equal area
set side by side. Sinan's central
plan contrasts with that of Haghia
Sophia; here the central dome is
buttressed by four semi-domes.
Süleyman later decided to build a
new sultanic mosque (the Süleymaniye) and consecrated the
Şehzade to the memory of his son
Mehmet, who died prematurely.

year he built a mosque in Aleppo. The Sultana Roxelana (Haseki Hürrem), Süleyman's favourite wife, put him to work in Istanbul in 1537 building a *külliye*. In 1539,
he was named chief architect of the court. He was already fifty years old.

The Şehzade: the First Sultanic Mosque

It was with the Şehzade that Sinan finally gave notice of his incomparable genius. It
is said that the name Şehzade – from the Persian *Shah Zadeh*, which means crown
prince – was given to the first great mosque built by Süleyman in memory of his
favourite son, Prince Mehmet. The date is disputed by scholars. The historian Ernst
Egli, author of a biography of Sinan, points out that building work began in 1543,
three months before the death of the heir apparent. Its construction must have
been decreed, and plans drawn up, months before; indeed, the site, overlooking
Istanbul between the Bayezit Camii and the Fatih Camii, had been cleared some
time before.

The roof of the Şehzade
By using a central plan, Sinan created a building that effectively presents the same system of roofing from every aspect. It is thus a sort of pyramid with the central dome as its summit. Here, one of the two minarets – the other is hidden by the dome – marks the junction of prayer-hall and courtyard.

The scale and position of the Şehzade exceed the requirements of commemoration, even that of a crown prince. Built on an esplanade 185 m long and 120 m wide, it measures 90 by 50 m (almost half a hectare). In its dimensions, the Şehzade is comparable to the Fatih Camii, which, at 96 by 56 m, was for many years the largest Ottoman building in Istanbul. The Şehzade should probably be regarded as Süleyman's first sultanic mosque.

It is an admirable architectural achievement. Sinan thought it his masterpiece, and it earned him the title of master builder (Turkish *mimar*). But even before the Şehzade was completed, in 1548, Süleyman seems to have ordered the construction of a new sultanic mosque. He wanted a building that would enhance his prestige and stand as an emblem of his reign, a point to which we shall return. At all events, two or three years later, work started on the Süleymaniye.

At this point, since a function was required for the superlative mosque then nearing completion, the sultan dedicated it to the memory of his son, who had died so young. The Şehzade thus remained a symbol of Süleyman's absolute power, and could serve, during the construction of the Süleymaniye, for the resplendent religious ceremonies attended by the ruler in his role as Sultan and Caliph.

The design of the Şehzade is again a product of the dialogue between Ottoman tradition and the Byzantine paradigm of Haghia Sophia. Two precedents influenced it. The first was the formula used by the architect Hayrettin for the Bayezit Camii in Istanbul: a central dome buttressed by two semi-domes at entrance and chevet to create a longitudinal nave. The second was Atik Sinan's design for the Fatih Camii, where omission of the frontal semi-dome allowed the creation of a traditional oblong prayer-hall.

Sinan's solution was a central dome 19 m in diameter and containing twenty-four windows buttressed by semi-domes (each with nine windows). He thus obtained a central plan with double trefoil. The central square is supported by large arches connected to the circle of the dome by smooth pendentives; the dome rests on four sturdy piers. The semi-domes forming the "apses" are flanked by a pair of squinches angled at forty-five degrees. At each of the four corners, smaller domes complete the diagonal symmetry. Finally, lateral galleries project from the sides of the building, where slender colonnettes support the arches of the open porticoes.

The result is a square central hall of unitary appearance. Seen from the exterior, the mosque presents a cascade of domes. On the north-west façade, these afford a seamless transition to the porticoed courtyard, which is also square, and comprises five domes on each of the four sides. Thus the pyramid-shaped mass of the prayer hall matches the "hollow" space of the portico, which forms the entrance to the mosque and frames the şadırvan.

The formula invented by Sinan is perfect. The architect achieved a hall that, with its furnishings (*dikka* and *minbar*), seems broader than it is deep, and thus meets the

A series of visible structures
To emphasise the oblong shape of the Şehzade's prayer-hall, which conformed to ancient Islamic tradition, the architect placed elegant galleries on the short sides of the oblong. The cylindrical towers form buttresses on the diagonal between the central dome and the corners of the prayer-hall.

A square courtyard

The broad elegant arcades of the porticoes in the Şehzade carry five domes on each side. Their width emphasises the slenderness of the monolithic columns. The *şadırvan* is sheltered by a kiosk resting on eight columns, like that of the Bayezit Camii in Istanbul.

requirements of an Islamic prayer-hall. On the other hand, the design makes the prayer-hall and courtyard equivalent, and their junction is marked by two minarets. The load-bearing qualities of the design are exceptional; it embodies harmonious distribution of thrust; all sides of the building are the same; no imbalance is possible. There are neither tympana, columns (reused or otherwise) nor any other heterogeneous elements to distract from the luminous, airy impression made by the building. The luminosity afforded by the many windows contrasts strongly with the shadowy interior of Haghia Sophia. The Şehzade undoubtedly possesses an imperial authority; it is an undeniably sultanic mosque, and its every detail is eloquent of its overall success.

A quatrefoil structure
This view of the roof of Sinan's
Şehzade shows the system of four
semi-domes buttressing the central dome, a structure combining
aesthetic unity with great
strength.

A transparent space
The structural clarity of the double
axial symmetry in the roof of the
Şehzade exhibits Sinan's mastery.
The central dome is only 19 m in
diameter and the keystone only
38 m above the paved floor, but
the building has a lightness and
grace that are quite remarkable.
This is particularly noticeable in
comparison with the Blue Mosque
(pages 200–201), which was built
sixty years later to a similar plan;
its heavy cylindrical piers have
nothing like the elegance of
Sinan's multi-faceted supports.

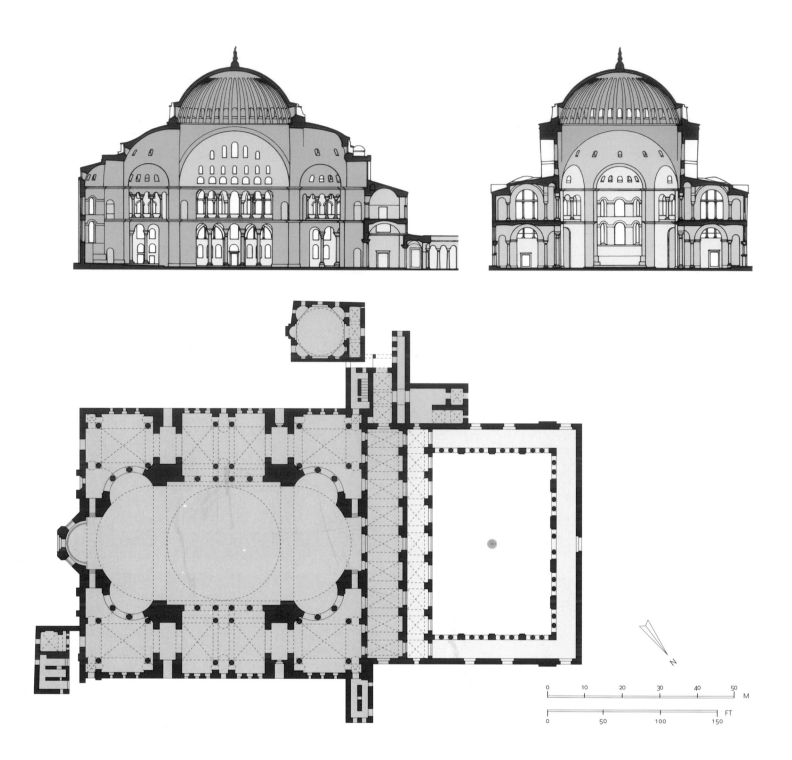

The Süleymaniye and its Byzantine Model

Work on the building of the Süleymaniye began on 15 June 1550, on a site once occupied by the Byzantine Capitol; the Old Palace had replaced it, and had itself been destroyed by fire in 1541. The site is a headland on the Golden Horn, and the *külliye* and mosque together cover an area of 350 by 280 m, or more than 8 hectares. The surface of the site is irregular, and the architect had to adapt the ordering of the *madrasas* and other buildings to the lie of the land. The sultanic mosque itself measures 108 by 73 m, and the highest point of its dome is 54 m. The *temenos* in which it is set measures, if we include the garden-cemetery and its *türbe*, 216 by 144 m.

For the Süleymaniye, Sinan returned to the basilican plan. The spaces created are like those of Haghia Sophia, with its central dome buttressed longitudinally by two semi-domes, and laterally by side-aisles behind the arcades that support the tym-

The paradigm

Longitudinal and transverse sections and plan of the basilica of Haghia Sophia at Constantinople. It was built in 532 by the architects Anthemios of Tralles and Isidorus of Miletus. The grandiose basilica of Justinian is a unique masterpiece, the greatest achievement of Roman building techniques and Byzantine art.

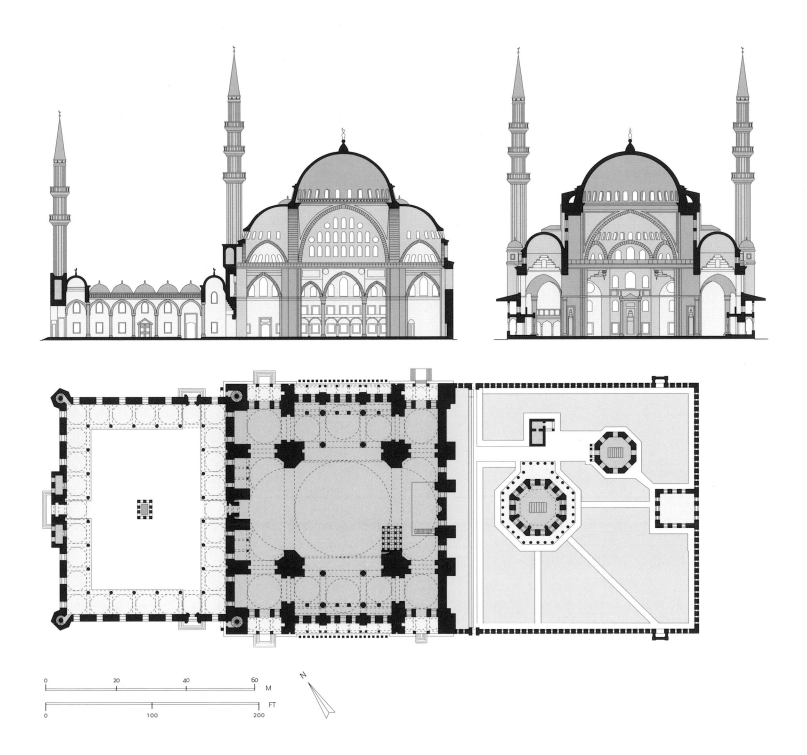

0 20 40 60 M
0 100 200 FT

N

An admirable interpretation
Longitudinal and transverse sections and plan of the Süleymaniye in Istanbul, begun in 1550 and designed by the architect Sinan. Though the basic design owes much to Haghia Sophia, it bears the hallmarks of Sinan's art.

pana. In Haghia Sophia, the side-aisles were cross-groined, with an upper gallery, whereas Sinan opted for domes. Both buildings have or had a courtyard; on the one hand, a Byzantine *atrium* (which has disappeared), on the other an Ottoman four-sided portico, which has seven domes on the short side, nine on the long; in both cases, the result is an oblong open space.

The two buildings are of similar dimensions, but the Süleymaniye is smaller overall. This has its own implications. Sinan was not, it seems, attempting to surpass Haghia Sophia, though he was capable of doing so, as he showed in the Selimiye at Edirne. Measurements make it clear that the parallel between the two buildings did not, as has often been thought, indicate a challenge on Sinan's part. Area at ground level: Haghia Sophia 140 by 72 m, Süleymaniye 108 by 73 m; nave length: 85 as against 65 m; diameter of the dome: 31 as against 27 m; height above floor-level: 56 as against 54 m; open courtyard space: 48 by 33 as against 46 by 32 m.

The domes of the Süleymaniye
This view of the roof structure
clearly shows Sinan's virtuosity.
The principal dome is 27 m in
diameter and has thirty-two lights
in its base; it rises to 54 m above
the paved floor. Via the four pendentives, it rests laterally on two
great arches above the tympana;
the arches are full of windows.
To the left and right, the granite
columns that support the
tympanum.

A revealing parallel
This transverse view of the Süleymaniye (above) shows the two semi-domes buttressing the central dome, and makes clear the analogies with the roof of Haghia Sophia (below), photographed at the same angle. In the Byzantine basilica, form flows into form; Sinan preferred to emphasise the constituent architectural elements.

The Süleymaniye and its prototype

Longitudinal view in the basilican space of the Süleymaniye (above), with its lateral tympana studded with windows, and its model, Haghia Sophia (below). In place of Haghia Sophia's arcaded lateral galleries, Sinan opened up large arches, thus establishing the continuity of the transverse space (the arches are visible in the bottom corners of the photograph).

sical columns, he established a physical connection with the pre-eminent tradition of Istanbul's past. These "allusions" function like quotations from classical authors in a contemporary text.

In Byzantium, and subsequently in Istanbul, Romano-Byzantine columns became mythologised. The legends attached to these splendid columns of pink Aswan granite (also known as porphyry, the imperial stone *par excellence*) imbued them with the prestige of mythical origins. Extraordinary stories were told of their provenance. In his *Constantinople Imaginaire*, a study of the collection of the *Patria*, the historian Gilbert Dagron gives an account of the myths surrounding the construction of Haghia Sophia and cites fables about the origin of the eight "Roman" columns, which were said to come from the Temple of Aurelian in Rome.

Ernest Mamboury cites a series of documents that refer to the four columns of the central hall of the Süleymaniye. One of them was known as the Column of Virginity, and had stood near the Church of the Holy Apostles; the second was thought to come from the Imperial Palaces, and had once supported a statue of the Emperor; the two others were said to have come from Alexandrette (now İskenderun).

Other legends, Byzantine and Ottoman, further enriched the significance of these columns. Some authors stated that they came from Hadrian's Temple at Cyzicus, which had been considered the eighth wonder of the world. Others saw in them relics of the Throne of Solomon, or of the cities of Ctesiphon and Haran, the land of Abraham, or even of Alexandria or Baalbek. In short, they constituted a guarantee of legitimacy in the form of a very physical heritage.

It was, therefore, as a symbolic embodiment of his position that Süleyman decreed the construction of this second sultanic mosque, one that was to eclipse the first through its symbolic importance. In the Şehzade, Sinan had shown the full measure of his talent; but he had not sought to integrate into its fabric the imperial legacy in which Süleyman now clothed himself as he contested the legitimacy of that other emperor, Charles V.

Muqarna **capitals**
The great columns of pink granite or porphyry that support the central square of the Süleymaniye have stalactite capitals and rings of gilded bronze as additional support against the enormous pressure that they bear.

Page 135
Süleyman's legendary columns
Standing between the central area and the side-aisles of the Süleymaniye, the monolithic columns of pink granite or porphyry are classical *spolia*. For Süleyman, their great significance was that they represented the tradition of empire. The prominence given to these Romano-Byzantine columns in the Süleymaniye symbolised his claim to the mantle of Justinian.

The Interpretation of Architecture

The interior of the Süleymaniye
Perspective view, looking towards the *mihrab*: the light that floods into the building (seen here from the imperial *loge*) transfigures architectural structures that, in Haghia Sophia, were bathed in reverential obscurity.

For many art historians, trained as philologists or at the Paris School of Palaeography and Librarianship (École des Chartes), architecture is to be interpreted exclusively through texts. This view embraces the logical absurdity that texts about a building are more meaningful than the building itself. To regard the primary sources as textual is to neglect the work in favour of the commentaries. Interpretation of the object itself then comes to be regarded as mere "intuition".

But architecture is its own language, with its own vocabulary, rules and syntax. Interpretation of a building must rely on a reading of the plan, and above all on first-hand acquaintance, just as archaeology depends on meticulous study of the site.

Textual interpretation, however, is very widespread, and clearly demonstrates the inadequacy of a historical methodology entirely dependent on documentation. We cannot too strongly state that comprehension of plan and elevation, spatial perception, and analysis of forms in their relation to more modern or more ancient monuments form the only reliable source. It is a source founded on direct perception, based on the language specific to architecture, and not on writings produced in reaction to that language.

Interpretation of this kind must inform any real re-evaluation of a work. It allows hypotheses to be adduced for which the evidence is the building itself, and to discern the motives that led to its nature and construction. It can reveal a meaning richer than the simple physical qualities of the object – *if* it can then be confirmed, by the philologist, from contemporary sources. It is at this point that the documentary specialist is called upon to confirm the interpretation of the building, through historical sources and traditional beliefs recorded in the archives.

The re-evaluation of the Süleymaniye's fundamental "meaning" given above is based on a complete reinterpretation of the building, which is restored to its original context and circumstances. Following a series of essays and publications on the subject of Sinan and Süleyman, the hypothesis that we have advanced here, and which we first put forward in 1985, has been confirmed by numerous Ottoman texts discovered by the scholar Stéphane Yerasimos. These documents confirm the accuracy of the approach described here, which is by no means simply a matter of "intuition"; it is the correct approach for the historian of architecture.

Harmonious forms
Seen from the height of the southern minaret, the virtuoso architectural repertory deployed by Sinan in the Süleymaniye: central dome, drum pierced with lights, and flying buttresses. Note in particular the powerful octagonal piers capped with ribbed domes that buttress the thrust of the main dome.

The Süleymaniye in Close-Up

The appearance of the Süleymaniye is in many respects different from that of Haghia Sophia. However, the comparison between the Byzantine basilica and Sinan's mosque requires us to restore certain features of the former. Thus, for example, the courtyard or *atrium* of the Haghia Sophia, which played an important role in the aesthetic composition of the building, no longer survives. And the awkward minarets added by the Muslims profoundly modify the external aspect of a building which should be judged on the basis of its internal space, rather than its silhouette – a silhouette that is, in the last analysis, somewhat squat and unsatisfying; the dome projects excessively and the vaults form a rather cumbersome and shapeless mass.

The Süleymaniye's lofty hemispherical dome is, by contrast, exceedingly graceful. Its elegance is enhanced by the four minarets at each corner of the courtyard, which delineate an empty space counterpoising the space occupied by the prayerhall. The beauty of the minarets, whose slender polygonal shafts attain heights of 63 and 81 m, testifies to Sinan's mastery. Their height is punctuated by galleries riding on stalactite vaulting.

Sinan generally preferred a slightly pointed arch to the semicircular Byzantine arch; the tension it imparts helps to lighten the structure. This is true of both the great internal arches carrying the dome and the porticoes that line the courtyard. The same concern for lightness is reflected in the use of stalactite work in the corners of the building, at the base of the vaults and at the top of columns, where the geometrical capitals are clothed in veritable *muqarnas*.

There are, it is true, notable influences from Italian Renaissance architecture in the lines of the Süleymaniye. This is particularly true of the *cyma recta* profile of the architraves, the spandrels of the arcades, and the carved bases of the courtyard columns, which feature *tori* and *scotiae* in the classical manner. But Sinan's work is nonetheless original. For example, the mouldings running horizontally along the top of the walls in places sometimes have a vertical downward extension to emphasise the continuity between one level and another. This is not a solution that classical architecture could ever have contemplated.

Finally, Sinan's work shows great honesty. The materials of the walls are always apparent, indeed, exalted for their purity and sobriety. The stonework, visible even from inside the prayer-hall, has been meticulously executed. The scarcely perceptible courses combine with the homogeneity of the limestone to give the impression of relief carved into a monolith, and the overall effect has the clarity of a diagram. This is in clear contrast with the polychrome revetments and mosaics that cover the walls of Haghia Sophia.

A Vast *külliye*

In addition to the precinct that encloses the *türbes* of Süleyman and Roxelana, his wife, the area covered by Sinan's sultanic complex comprises the usual *külliye* buildings. Because the land slopes down on either hand so that the "platform" of the *külliye* forms an irregular diamond-shape, the orientation of the buildings is set by the mosque.

With the exception of the baths or *hammams*, the layout remains rectilinear, but is not axial. Seen from the top of one of the Süleymaniye minarets, the flocks of domes outline the many courtyards. To the east and west are five *madrasas*; to the north is a hospital-dispensary, an *imaret* – people's refectory – and a bookshop-cum-library. These low buildings for the most part have a central porticoed courtyard from which one reaches the multi-domed halls or individual cells.

Harmoniously set out among the full-grown trees and the lawns surrounding the mosque, the Süleymaniye complex is a dazzling architectural achievement. Whatever its message, Sinan's work for Süleyman gives the full measure of a prodigiously gifted architect. Süleyman's close and trusting relationship with Sinan was vital to the creation of this complex, which has few if any contemporaneous rivals in the West. Is there a single Renaissance artist who could boast of designing and implementing a project on this scale?

One factor in the swift completion of the complex was the reliable funding available to Sinan. Construction took less than ten years. The *Annals* of Topkapı tell us that 2 500 workers, Christian and Muslim (all of them waged, none conscripted) laboured on the site, and that they worked 5 500 000 man-days.

A clean outline

One of the characteristics of Sinan's style lies in the crisp outline of his buildings – here the Süleymaniye –, in particular the mouldings which emphasise the coping of the walls and such elements of transition as *muqarnas* or stalactites. The rainspouts have a sober and well-defined form, showing a kind of precocious functionalism.

Gallery entrances

The organisation of the walls and windows of the Süleymaniye provides for external galleries between the powerful buttresses; they serve as elegant secondary entrances.

Purity of line

The spandrel separating the gallery arches is adorned with a disc of porphyry; the scheme matches the alternating dark and light stone of the voussoirs. A classical moulding runs above this austere decoration. The effect is reminiscent of Brunelleschi's Spedale degli Innocenti in Florence (1421–1424), Laurana's Palazzo Ducale at Urbino (*circa* 1465), or even the Palazzo della Cancelleria in Rome (1485–1511). It is possible that Sinan was influenced in the design of these spandrels (and in his use of other Renaissance formulae) by the Italian painters resident at the Topkapı court.

Tripartite organisation
The external galleries in the Süleymaniye display a mixture of rigorous logic and creative freedom. The portico is surmounted by a large pointed arch and comprises three arches, the outside arches merging into the walls. To the left and right, therefore, the discs ornamenting the spandrels are cut in half. By contrast, the door is placed in the last arcade to the right (or left in another example), in defiance of symmetry.

Lacework in stone
A detail of the external gallery balustrade of the Süleymaniye. The tracery of the marble *claustra* is based on a six-pointed star motif.

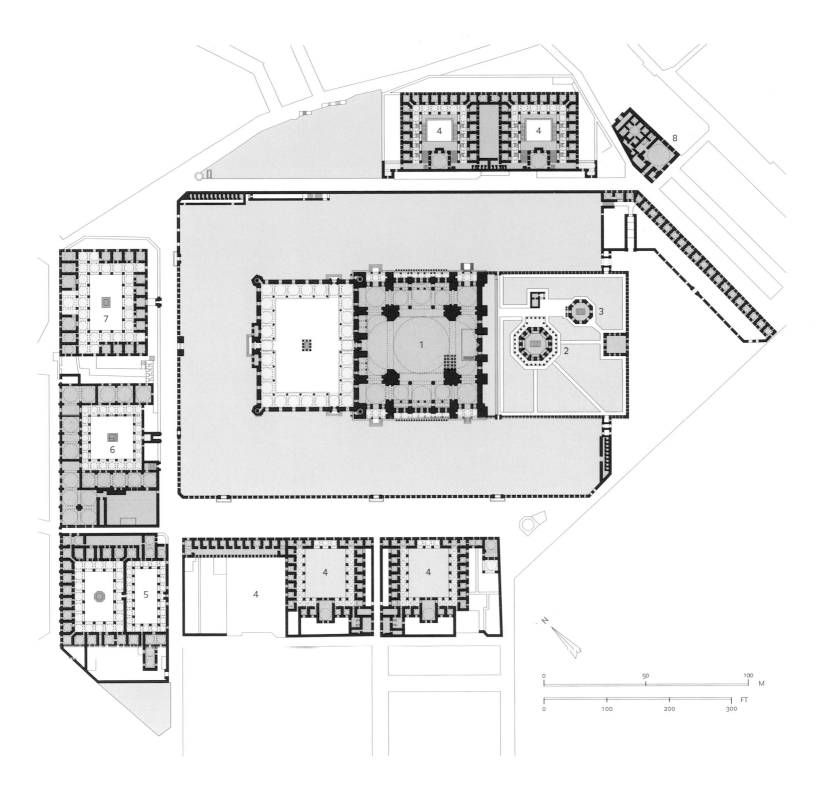

The *külliye* of Süleyman

The sultan's foundation is regular in layout. The plan had to accommodate the lie of the land; the Süleymaniye stands on a steep slope.

1 Mosque
2 *Türbe* of Süleyman
3 *Türbe* of the Sultana Haseki Hürrem
4 *Madrasa*
5 Hospital-dispensary
6 *Imaret* or popular refectory
7 Library
8 *Hammam* or baths

Welcoming the faithful
The faithful who travel to the Süleymaniye are accommodated in the four *madrasas* bordering the open spaces of the *külliye*. Their porticoed courtyards are roofed with rows of domes, whose regularity is emphasised by the tall chimneys.

A haven of tranquillity
The arcades in the courtyard of the Süleymaniye are of differing heights, creating a peaceful rhythm in the space before the prayer-hall.

A double *hammam*
The baths of the Sultana Haseki Hürrem (Roxelana) in Istanbul were designed for equal numbers of men and women. The symmetrical composition is clearly expressed in the layout of the domes.

Engineering Works

Sinan employed this impressive workforce of quarrymen, masons, stonecarvers, workmen and specialists in public works of all kinds; in his role as architect-in-chief to the court, he was a kind of Minister of Works. One such category of work was the "architecture of water": aqueducts and *hammams*. Intended to improve the living standards of the citizens of Istanbul, these accounted for much of the construction work of the mid-sixteenth century.

Among Sinan's feats of hydraulic engineering was the capital's network of aqueducts. In the century of its life as the Ottoman capital, Istanbul had become a busy and populous metropolis, and its water requirements had greatly increased. Quantities of fountains (the *sebil* was a fixture in places of worship) and *hammams* had been built: these institutions needed large volumes of water, which were sometimes transported over considerable distances by aqueduct.

Provision of water on a scale to match the population and new institutions of Istanbul led to a twofold effort. On the one hand, the Romano-Byzantine aqueducts, such as the Valens aqueduct, were systematically restored. On the other, new projects were begun in the north-east of the town in order to span a low-lying area called Belgrade Forest. One of these new aqueducts, whose Turkish name is Uzunkemer ("long aqueduct"), dates from 1563, and consists of two tiers of arcades 716 m long and 26 m high. Another, the Eğrikemer ("bent aqueduct"), is 342 m long and has three tiers of arcades carrying a watercourse 35 m above the ground. These two works are fine engineering feats, with bossaged stones and semicircular arches.

These works ensured the water supply of the *hammams* of Istanbul. One *hammam* was designed by Sinan and stands opposite Haghia Sophia. Built at the command of the Sultana Roxelana, it is the *hammam* of Haseki Hürrem (her Turkish name), con-

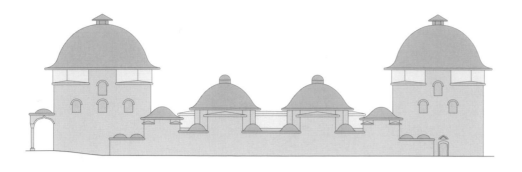

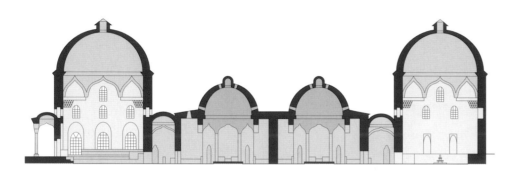

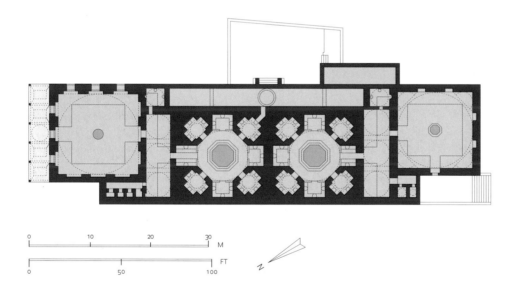

structed in 1556, and has just been handsomely restored. It was conceived as a symmetrical whole, one side for men, the other for women. It comprises (in order from the outside) vestibule with pool, a steam bath under an octagonal dome, and a rest room with cabins for massage, depilation and cosmetic functions. All of these are domed halls, and all of them are duplicated on the other side. As tradition required, the domed spaces have little openings in the leaded roof, glazed with solid bell-shaped glass inserts.

Among Sinan's public works, we should also mention the Tekke of Süleyman at Damascus. The word *tekkiye* or *tekke* refers to a convent for dervishes, but in this case the building was intended to accommodate pilgrims on their way to Mecca. This *külliye*, founded in 1553, occupies a huge area around 100 by 150 m, at the back of which rises a handsome single-domed mosque flanked by two minarets; it has a four-column vestibule and a projecting canopy supported on twelve columns, two

A staging-post on the pilgrimage
to Mecca
The Tekke of Süleyman at Damascus on the road south to
Mecca is a dervish convent which
acts as a staging-post. It was built
by Sinan in 1553 – at the same
time as the Süleymaniye in Istanbul – and includes a mosque. The
decoration of the prayer-hall is
geometrical and derives from
Ayyubid and Mamluk art. A single
dome on pendentives covers the
square hall.

Sinan's Originality

The considerable workforce that had been gathered by Sinan at Istanbul for the construction of the Şehzade and the Süleymaniye was soon set to work on a similar project. For this, Sinan took up his innovations at the point at which he had been forced
by Süleyman's orders to abandon them. The symbolic significance that Süleyman
sought to bestow on the Süleymaniye had prevented Sinan from following his own
instincts and distancing himself from the model of Haghia Sophia. Now he could
return to his quest.

Around the middle of the sixteenth century, the Grand Vizier Ahmet Paşa commissioned him to build a mosque close to the Land Wall, halfway between Marmara
and the Golden Horn. The work had a troubled history: Sinan's patron was put to
death in 1555, and the mosque, the Kara Ahmet Paşa Camii, was completed some
ten years later, on a somewhat smaller scale than originally planned, as funds were
by then lacking.

The distinctive aspect of this design is the hexagonal dome flanked by four semi-
domes; the overall effect is like a baldachin set into an oblong hall 28 by 18 m. The
six corners of the dome rest on reused classical columns in red granite, with magnificent stalactite capitals.

The homogeneity of the internal space (some 20 m high) thus created, without
any support other than the peripheral columns, is a remarkable technical and aesthetic achievement. The buttressing is formed by a system of double walls that
leaves the *qibla* wall perfectly vertical. This is a considerable advance on the "cascade" of domes forming a pyramidal mass leading down from the summit to the
base of the roof.

Sinan returned to the formula of a commanding central dome in the remarkable
mosque dedicated to Princess Mihrimah, Süleyman's daughter, which stands not far
from the Edirne Gate. Work began after the death of Mihrimah in 1558, and is
thought to have been completed between 1562 and 1565. It was a genuinely audacious project. This time, the dimensions of the oblong prayer-hall were 22 by 33 m,
and the summit of the dome was 38 m above the paved floor.

The plan shows an oblong *haram* preceded by a vast porticoed courtyard, which
is substantially wider on both sides than the prayer-hall. On either side of the central dome are three small domes, which made it possible for tribunes to be set above
the side-aisles. The *qibla* supports a tympanum with its own openings. On either

Page 151
Polychrome masonry
In the Tekke of Süleyman at Damascus, the alternating courses of
light and dark stone (*ablaq* work)
derive from an Arabic tradition
adopted by the Selçuks. The cubic
building is surmounted by a hemispherical dome with flying buttresses; it has two handsome
minarets, each with a single
gallery. The volumetrics of the
building are typical of Sinan's
manner.

The Kara Ahmet Paşa Camii
Built in Istanbul between 1550 and 1562, the mosque, named after Süleyman's Grand Vizier, is hexagonal in plan. The principal dome, buttressed by two pairs of large squinches, rests on handsome reused classical columns of pale red granite. The mosque possesses a particularly fine marble *minbar* with lattice-work panels.

Trees in the mosque courtyard

View from above of the oblong
court of the Mihrimah Camii in
Istanbul. This mosque has double
lateral porticoes, with two rows
of small domes. In the centre of
the courtyard, a kiosk shelters
the *şadırvan*.

Invisible buttressing

Plan and longitudinal section of
the Mihrimah Camii, built by Sinan
and completed in 1565. It has an
oblong plan with a central dome
riding on eight supports: four reused classical columns, two at
each of the short sides, and four
piers built into the front and back
walls. The elevation shows that
the mosque has no visible buttressing to counter the thrust of
its dome, which is 22 m in diameter
and attains a height of 32 m.

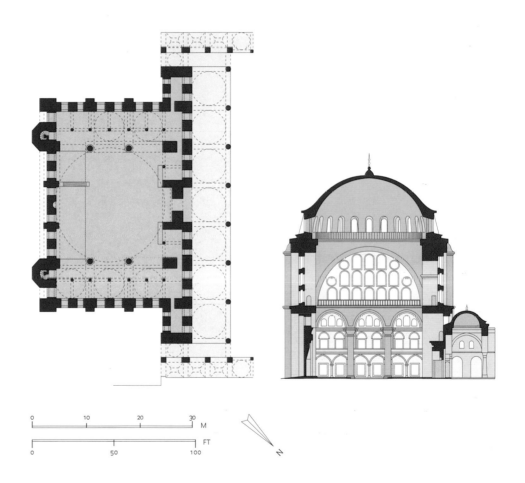

A light-filled interior

The Şehzade followed the paradigm of Haghia Sophia and used four semi-domes to buttress the central dome. Sinan's Mihrimah adopts another component of his illustrious model, the tympana, which are here used on all four walls of the mosque. Sinan's audacity was rewarded with a luminous, crystalline interior.

Transparent walls

The miracle of the Mihrimah Camii lies not only in its lack of buttressing, but in the number of windows set into the walls sustaining the dome. There are nineteen windows in the *mihrab* and nineteen more in the tympanum, making a total of thirty-eight in the *qibla* as a whole. The base of the dome adds a further twenty-four lights.

Page 155

Uncompromising verticality

The chevet of the Mihrimah Camii in Istanbul presents a façade as sheer as a cliff-face, made up of a single great arch between the octagonal corner-piers that buttress the thrust of the dome. The architect, Sinan, demonstrates here his extreme virtuosity.

The Culminating Achievements of Sinan Under Selim II

The Selimiye at Edirne

Page 159

Glittering colours in stained glass
At Üsküdar, on the bank of the Bosphorus opposite Istanbul, Sinan built an earlier mosque bearing the name of the Princess Mihrimah. The splendid stained-glass windows are framed in stucco.

Tribute money
This miniature from the *Hünername* of Sultan Murat III (1574–1595) shows Sultan Mehmet receiving gold tribute from his subjects. Painted by Osman in 1584, this superlative work is organised on three levels. In the lowest, the gold is collected, in the centre it is deposited before the sultan, and in the top level the sovereign himself, seated in his state tent, surveys the scene. (Library of the Topkapı Sarayı Museum, Istanbul)

By the time of Süleyman's death, Ottoman architecture had attained its apogee in Sinan's ever more inventive designs, realised in a series of exceptionally fine buildings. The inauguration of the Selimiye at Edirne found Sinan an old man of eighty-five, but in full possession of his faculties. He revolutionised architecture, contriving to exceed in every respect the limits by which his nonetheless remarkable predecessors had been confined. The basilican plans that they had preferred were replaced by central plans affording incomparable lightness and harmony.

We now turn our attention to the masterpieces that he built after 1566; they offer a spectacular illustration of his mastery, reflecting his increasingly complex techniques. We start with the Sokollu Mehmet Paşa Camii in Istanbul, which dates from 1570–1572, and go on to the Azapkapı Camii in Istanbul, inaugurated in 1577, and finally (in terms of technique) to the Selimiye in Edirne, completed in 1574.

The first two mosques were commissioned by the Grand Vizier Sokollu Mehmet Paşa, who occupied the highest post in the Ottoman court hierarchy from 1565 to 1579, when he was assassinated. Mehmet Paşa was of Bosnian origin and a Christian by birth; he was already the director of Ottoman affairs during the last year of Süleyman's reign, and held office throughout the reign of Selim II (1566–1574) and during part of the reign of Murat II (1574–1595). The smooth transition of power in the difficult circumstances surrounding Süleyman's death was to a large extent owed to the role played by Sokollu. Süleyman was laying siege to Szeged (in modern Hungary) when he died while commanding a Turkish camp comprising 90 000 men and 300 cannons. Selim's accession to power is one of the most dramatic moments in the history of the Ottoman dynasty.

The Grand Vizier did not reveal the death of the Sultan to his entourage, and pretended still to be following his master's orders. He had, meanwhile, informed Selim, who travelled for forty-three days from Kütahya in Anatolia in order to assume his late father's throne. The deaths earlier of Süleyman's other sons, Mustafa and Bayezit, both of whom were undoubtedly more capable than Selim, meant that the heir apparent was a drunkard surrounded by courtesans, and the reins of power remained in the Vizier's hands.

Sokollu Mehmet Paşa retained Sinan as the court's architect in chief, and, indeed, commissioned the two mosques with which he endowed the capital. The interest of these two works, neither of them on a monumental scale, lies in the new techniques that Sinan used in their construction.

The Sokollu and the Azapkapı Camii at Istanbul
The Mihrimah Camii, with its single dome on a square base carried by four corner piers and linked to the base of the dome by smooth triangular pendentives of spherical section, had been Sinan's most revolutionary building up to this time. In the Sokollu Camii, he returned to the hexagonal formula of the Kara Ahmet Paşa Camii of fifteen years before. But he contrived to give to the central dome and two pairs

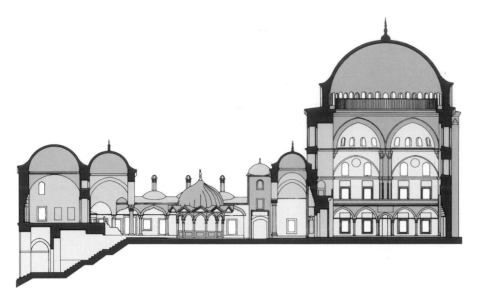

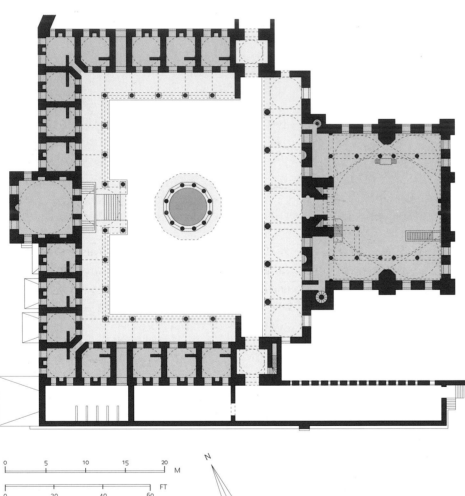

The Sokollu Mehmet Paşa Camii
Longitudinal section and plan of
the mosque built by the Grand
Vizier Mehmet Paşa Sokollu at
Istanbul in 1570. From the
entrance, on the left, the courtyard is reached via an under-
ground passage. The mosque
itself has a hexagonal dome with
four great lateral squinches, and
surges up unsupported like the
Mihrimah.

Page 163 above
Courtyard and kiosk
The visitor emerging into the
courtyard of the Sokollu Mehmet
Paşa Camii in Istanbul discovers a
space bounded by porticoes, a
şadırvan kiosk at its centre and
the prayer-hall rising above it.

0   5   10   15   20
                              M
0   20   40   60
                   FT

N

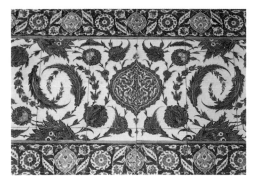

Ceramic revetment

The interior of the Sokollu
Mehmet Paşa Camii is adorned
with a superb revetment of İznik
tiling in vivid colours, showing
classical Turkish motifs.

of lateral semi-domes a greater unity and spatial coherence. This comes principally from a greater elevation. Sinan reverted here to the hexagonal dome; its 120-degree angles soften the transition from one surface to another. This produces greater unity between the centre of the prayer-hall and its lateral extensions, and Sinan thus obtained an effect of admirable homogeneity.

Built on sloping ground, downhill from the Hippodrome and not far from the Bosphorus, the Sokollu Mehmet Paşa Camii reserves a surprise for the visitor. The access to the 85 by 65 m precinct enclosing the *külliye* and mosque, with its porticoed courtyard, is gained by a staircase that forms a kind of tunnel. This passage links the entrance, which is at the lowest point of the site, to the courtyard eight metres above, passing under the buildings of the *tekkiye*. The visitor emerges from the passage to find himself in a courtyard surrounded by arcades giving on to individual cells and confronted by the mosque's sunlit façade as though by full daylight. The mosque has a seven-domed vestibule and a portal in stalactite work capped by a dome whose *intrados* is covered in İznik tiles.

Stepping through the threshold, the visitor is astonished by the apparent size of the oblong prayer-hall, despite its modest dimensions: 14 by 18 m, and 25 m high at the keystone. The *qibla* is covered in tiles displaying blue flowers on a white background, over which the tympanum is lit by two rows of three polychrome windows.

To each side, the architect has provided for internal galleries, capped with the pairs of semi-domes that flank the arches of the hexagon. Note that the pendentives of the lateral structures are covered with stalactite work. A large pillar on the transversal axis of the hall supports the springing of the arches. The six smooth

A splendid porch
Despite its small scale, the Sokollu Mehmet Paşa Camii in Istanbul is richly decorated. Its entrance combines inscriptions and stalactite niches; its dome rests on *muqarna* pendentives and is covered in polychrome tiling.

Page 165

A polychrome prayer-hall
The oblong space of the Sokollu Mehmet Paşa Camii in Istanbul has an exceptional feature: the *qibla*, with its sober *mihrab* and stone *minbar*, has a polychrome tile revetment, as do the squinches supporting the dome. Windows are let into the upper part of the walls. The lateral galleries, normally reserved for women, contribute to the definition of the central space.

pendentives of the central dome are decorated with İznik tiles, and at its base are twenty windows. Indeed, the many windows in the mosque, from the dome downwards, flood it with light.

The Sokollu Camii demonstrated the spatial homogeneity that could be achieved by the use of a hexagonal dome. Though the tradition of the oblong prayer-hall is maintained, here, for the first time in Islamic architecture, the vertical is accorded a particular emphasis. In short, the Sokollu mosque marks a break with the tradition of both the Şehzade and the Süleymaniye. It illustrates the new possibilities that found their full expression in the Selimiye in Edirne, which also makes use of a hexagonal plan.

Among the various designs with which Sinan experimented, the octagonal plan had a particular merit, that of allowing the architect to alternate axial apses and diagonal squinches. The Azapkapı Camii in Istanbul illustrates this device clearly. Sited on the Galata side of the Golden Horn, opposite the Süleymaniye, this mosque

A traditional bouquet
Chrysanthemums, carnations and cornflowers are the motifs featured on the exquisite tile revetment of the Sokollu Mehmet Paşa Camii in Istanbul, which dates from 1570–1572.

The invention of space
The mosque of the Grand Vizier Sokollu, who held the reins of power in the court of Selim II. The mosque marks a high point in Sinan's exploration of the hexagonal plan; a unified internal space is obtained with a perfect balance of forms, from which every notion of thrust and weight is banished.

Late experiments
The mosques of the Ottoman viziers and *paşas* offered Sinan, late in his life, almost endless possibilities for experiment. The octogenarian architect continued to renew his language and hone his formal accomplishments. In the Azapkapı Camii, designed in 1577, Sinan returned to the octagonal plan. He contrived to buttress the dome by using a double shell, thus constructing lateral passages like those in the Selimiye at Edirne (see page 175 right).

was intended for the workers in the shipyards. It is of relatively modest dimensions. The highest point of the hall is 17.5 m and its longest sides are 23 m. At the back of this oblong space, the *mihrab* constitutes a kind of apse. The load of the single dome is distributed between the two large piers that frame this apse and six octagonal columns. It is held up by a crown of pointed arches. It thus forms a small-scale variant of the formula adopted in the Selimiye at Edirne, though it lacks that building's authority and does not possess the sense of self-evident rightness that informs the Selimiye.

Page 169

The apotheosis of the octagon
Construction of the Selimiye in Edirne began in 1567, but it was not finished until 1574. In it, Sinan perfected his technique and created the greatest masterpiece of Ottoman art. The four minarets are 82 m high.

Hemisphere and cylinder
The fluted minarets of the Selimiye at Edirne, with their delicate galleries on stalactite corbels, keep guard over the gilded copper finial on the summit of the dome.

The Design of the Selimiye

Since Süleyman died only in 1566, and work began on the Selimiye at Edirne at the latest in 1567, it seems likely that Sinan's design had already been sketched out before circumstances allowed him to realise it. It was in Edirne, 225 km to the north-west of the capital, that the opportunity arose. For the Ottomans, the importance of this city was as a citadel close to the front line of their Hungarian campaign. The Selimiye was to be a standard-bearer of Islam.

The year 1568 was one in which the further advance of Turkish power could be celebrated. A treaty was signed with the Emperor Maximilian II in which he bound himself to pay Selim II an annual tribute of 30 000 golden ducats. And an embassy was received from Persia, similarly anxious to obtain a peace treaty.

The important role occupied by Edirne in the policy of the Sublime Porte thus merited the construction of a sultanic mosque. Work went on apace, paid for by the spoils of war and by tribute money; by 1572 the arches supporting the dome had

The quest for unity
Longitudinal section of the
Selimiye at Edirne. Sinan created
a homogeneous prayer-hall of
great spatial density beneath the
enormous central dome.

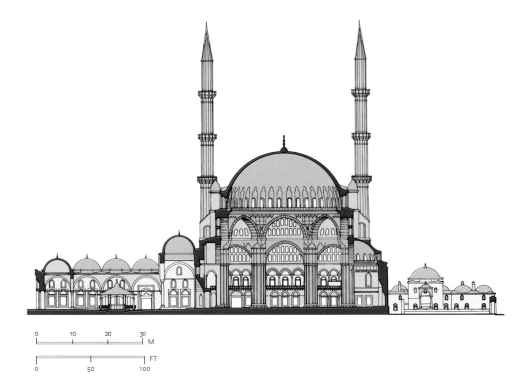

Mastery of space
With the Selimiye, Sinan achieved
all his ambitions. The domed
prayer-hall with its central plan
owes nothing to the architecture
of Haghia Sophia. The internal
diameter of the dome is 31.5 m
and its highest point is 44 m above
the floor. It is thus slightly larger
than that of Haghia Sophia. More
significant than its dimensions is
the coherence of the space it creates (see also pages 18–19).

been completed, and in 1573 the dome was in place. The inauguration took place the following year.

The Selimiye stands on a rise in an oblong *temenos* 200 by 110 m; in the centre of the precinct stands the mosque with the courtyard, and on the eastern corners of the mosque, at the *qibla* end, are two square *madrasas*. Around 1580, the architect Da'ud Ağa completed the *külliye* with a bazaar, which runs along the long, southern side of the complex. Da'ud Ağa was a pupil of Sinan's who worked under Murat III (1574–1595).

At Edirne, Sinan chose to make the load-bearing structure still more coherent than in his previous buildings, and to emphasise the compact volume and the symmetry of its components by placing four extraordinarily slender minarets on each side of the central dome; the contrast accentuates the vertical mass of the building. Sinan thus imparted a powerful vertical dynamic to the building, and, by making use

The Selimiye at Edirne and its *külliye*

Plan of the Selim II foundation in Edirne. In the centre, the mosque and courtyard known as the Selimiye; the oblong courtyard and the prayer-hall are identical in area. The octagonal prayer-hall is formed by a building 66 by 50 m buttressed by the four minarets. To the right are two courtyard *madrasas*; at the bottom of the plan is the bazaar built around 1580 by Sinan's pupil, Da'ud Ağa.

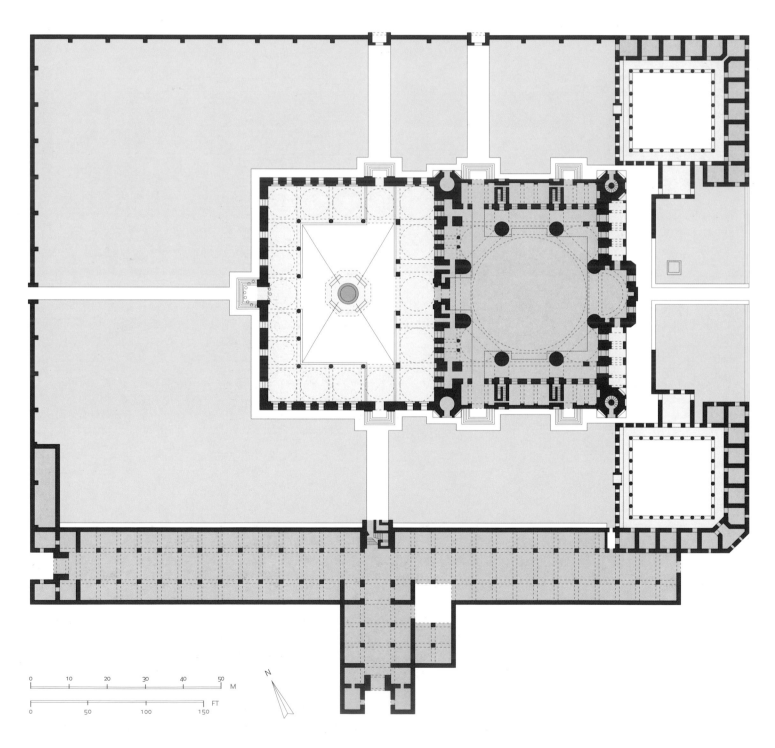

A perfectly balanced structure
The dome of the Selimiye of
Edirne is framed by the minarets
at the four corners of the building.
The eight corner piers define the
structure of the central dome.
Tympana and squinches alternate
on two different levels of the
façade.

of the minarets as buttressing piers, he combined immense structural efficiency
with pronounced vertical emphasis.

The entire building is 100 m long and 68 m wide; the prayer-hall is 35 m deep and
46 m wide. The highest point of the dome, measured from the paved floor, is 44 m.
The load of the dome is carried by an octagonal base on eight piers, cross-braced by
half-dome squinches some 12 m in diameter. This allowed Sinan to dispense with
the large pendentives that he had used elsewhere, and to create a structure that
offered a greater sense of space within the conventional oblong internal space. The
prayer-hall thus gained in unity.

True, there are pendentives at the angles linking the octagon to the circular
base of the dome, and at the base of the four large corner squinches. But they are
disguised by the stalactite work that covers them. The dome is 31.5 m in diameter,
thus exceeding that of Haghia Sophia by half a metre – though the latter is 12 m
higher and rests on only four piers. Once again, we note, Sinan did not treat Haghia
Sophia as a challenge; he did not seek to eclipse its architects Anthemios of Tralles
and Isidorus of Miletus. Instead, his object was to elaborate a new form of roofing, in which the central dome does not require buttressing semi-domes or side-
aisles. By contrast with Haghia Sophia, on the four axial faces of the octagon and
at the corners of the hall, tympana pierced with windows bring in still further
light, in addition to that admitted by the thirty-two windows in the base of the
dome.

In the Mihrimah, Sinan had created a prayer-hall flooded with light. To an even
greater extent, the Selimiye is a transparent shell; there are more than 270 win-

Cascading forms
Among the characteristics of Sinan's architecture are the cascades of domes and the use of flying buttresses to contain the thrust of the main dome. Here, the successive structural elements culminate in the dome of the Selimiye.

dows. Illuminated in this way, the prayer-hall seems a weightless structure of a limpid, almost intangible kind. This is architecture of the very highest quality; even the Western Renaissance is hard-pressed to offer a comparable mastery of the art.

How did Sinan resolve the problems of thrust generated by the weight of the dome? The key to Sinan's structure (indeed, to his architectonic language) is the internal buttressing-walls, which led him to create a double-shell system. One manifestation of this is the galleries that surround the prayer-hall and pass behind the main piers. They create a discreet form of internal buttressing so perfectly integrated into the shape of the building that their function is imperceptible and disappears into the overall structure.

The unity of the prayer-hall is striking. There is no subdivision to disturb the serene, transparent space, which consequently gives a monolithic impression. It is the product of astonishing virtuosity. Further confirmation of Sinan's accomplish-

The technique of "double shell" buttressing practised by Sinan finds its most brilliant application in the Selimiye. Thus the internal pier (left) placed at one of the corners of the octagon is reinforced by an enormous flying buttress. This function is masked by the lateral galleries and the passage that runs beneath the vault.

Flower and vine-leaf
As in the Sokollu Mehmet Paşa Camii in Istanbul, the Selimiye in Edirne exhibits handsome tile revetments on which intertwined floral motifs proliferate.

ment comes in the internal rhythms: the play of mass and volume in the piers of the octagon, which are surmounted by pinnacles, and in the numerous tympana under large, slightly pointed arches. The Selimiye moreover exhibits a vigorous and largely unopposed vertical dynamic.

As in the Şehzade, the surface area of the porticoed courtyard is equal to that of the prayer-hall. But here, both areas are square rather than oblong. The courtyard has seven domes along the entrance side, five on each side, and five larger domes contiguous with the prayer hall. In its centre is a sixteen-sided marble *şadırvan*. The columns are capped with stalactite capitals and carry elegant porticoes. Opposite the prayer-hall, Sinan chose a symmetrical rhythm based on two pairs of columns which frame the entrance. The fact is noteworthy because the same pattern features in many Christian churches, its Solomonic symbolism referring to the notion of the Temple. Was Sinan influenced by this, as in the Süleymaniye? The same choice

Rhythmic contrast
In the rear façade of the Selimiye at Edirne, Sinan imitated the alternating thicknesses of the flying buttresses in his design for the arcades. The relatively narrow arches of the façade thus contrast with the broad arches of the porticoes. The narrower arches and paired columns produce a springy rhythm.

Sculptural details
The capitals of the Selimiye at Edirne play variations on the *muqarna* theme; the rigorously sculptural treatment makes considerable aesthetic impact.

A peaceful courtyard
The wide arches of the courtyard porticoes suggest a classical tranquillity further emphasised by the slenderness of the columns.

Alternating arches
The main entrance of the Selimiye in Edirne reverts to the twin columns and shorter arches of the rear façade. Note the four-centred profile of the shorter arches and the use of white marble discs marking the height of the wider arches. The pairs of columns framing the entrance bear a symbolic reference to the Temple of Solomon. In the foreground, the *şadırvan*.

is made in the galleries that flank the chevet of the prayer-hall, on either side of the apse housing the *mihrab*.

Sinan still had eleven of his ninety-five years to live when he built what is undoubtedly his masterpiece. It combines an entirely logical central plan with an originality that revolutionised the language of architecture. In this, he went quite beyond the grasp of his contemporaries. The Selimiye marks the furthest point of Sinan's originality, and his successors, who were also his pupils, did not pursue the logic it implied. They failed to grasp the visionary old man's quest for ever greater coherence, grace and luminosity.

Sinan's was a life of prodigious accomplishment; he never rested on his laurels and was never content with his own achievements. It was as if he were determined to demonstrate the unquenchable resources of the imagination. At the age of ninety-five he decided to fulfil the ritual obligation of the *haj* or pilgrimage. He returned safe and sound, bearing the title (*hajj*) awarded to those who have accomplished their duty as Muslims by travelling to the Holy Places, Medina and Mecca, and circumambulating the Kaaba, the Black Stone, which, as the tradition records, was bestowed on Abraham by Gabriel.

The Fındıklı Camii
This little mosque, in Istanbul, stands on the edge of the Bosphorus. Rightly attributed to Sinan, it is dated to 1565 and forms part of the master-architect's research into the spatial possibilities offered by the central plan. But it also reveals a certain clumsiness, suggesting that Sinan did not himself oversee the construction.

A design disfigured
The errors of the site overseer at the Fındıklı Camii are clear in this photograph: the lack of capitals disfigures the junction of arches and piers.

Composite whole
Seen from the outside, the Fındıklı Camii nonetheless shows a harmonious arrangement of volumes that is entirely characteristic of Sinan, and confirms the attribution.

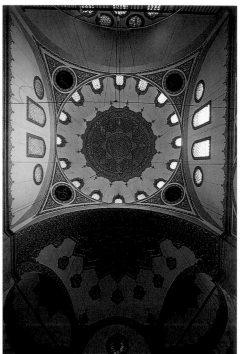

Late Sinan and After Sinan

In addition to these outstandingly successful and innovative buildings, Sinan gave
his name to more traditional and less accomplished buildings. It seems that the old
master was willing to delegate responsibility for some of these, allowing a degree
of initiative to his "public works enterprise". His studio assistants produced numerous buildings over which Sinan merely cast his supervisor's eye. This is the case with
a number of mosques; one such is the Fındıklı Camii, on the shores of the Bosphorus, which was built in 1565. Though its hexagonal formula is not without interest,
it exhibits certain undeniable defects.

Among these "standard" productions, if the world may be used without pejor-
ative intent, is the Selimiye in Konya, the former Selçuk capital. Built near the convent of the whirling dervishes, it has a façade with a fine gallery-vestibule, whose
seven-arched arcade is framed by two minarets. The mosque is square in plan, and,
capped with a single dome on pendentives, it offers an almost cubic silhouette. At
ground level, it has side-aisles and a deep apse flanked by two squinches; the *mihrab*
is at the back of the apse. This mosque bears all the hallmarks of Sinan's art. In its
lines, in its re-entrant curves topped with stalactite-work squinches, and its mouldings, which run now horizontally, now vertically, in order to unify the body of the
building, the hand of the master is evident.

The Kılıç Ali Paşa Camii, built in 1582 in the Tophane quarter of Istanbul on the
shores of the Bosphorus, is, by contrast, a curious exception to the steady development of Sinan's art. It was commissioned by Kılıç Ali, the Admiral of the Turkish fleet,

Classical ornament

In the Selimiye at Konya, the outline of the building is given a characteristic Sinan treatment. The details here are similar to those of the Süleymaniye at Istanbul (see page 140).

A harmonious elevation

The façade of the Selimiye at Konya – its elegant entrance portico forming seven arches, its two very sober minarets and the cubic outline of its prayer-hall, capped with a dome – illustrates Sinan's aspiration to clarity in the absence of innovation.

Analogies with Haghia Sophia
The Kılıç Ali Paşa Camii in Istanbul was built in 1582 in the Tophane quarter in Galata, opposite the Topkapı. It is often attributed to Sinan, but the architectural scheme here is in complete contrast to the experiments conducted by Sinan late in his life. With its tympana and buttressing semi-domes, the building is clearly a small-scale version of Haghia Sophia, and should therefore be ascribed to one of Sinan's assistants.

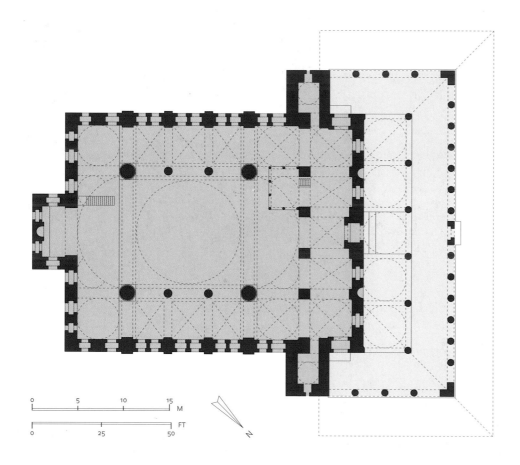

More tradition than innovation
The plan of the Kılıç Ali Paşa Camii is directly inspired by the Byzantine basilica of Haghia Sophia. It rests on four great pillars which support the central square; the dome is buttressed by wide semi-domes. The entrance portico is covered by broad projecting eaves.

Decagonal star motifs
Detail of a shutter panel in the
Kılıç Ali Paşa Camii in Istanbul.
The various decagonal figures
and the light inlays combine in
a pellucid composition.

The Byzantine model
A perspective view of the nave
of the Kılıç Ali Paşa Camii. It immediately suggests a small-scale version of its model, Haghia Sophia:
side-aisles, lateral galleries, and
tympana under a dome on pendentives. While its design is not
original, the building exhibits
superlative attention to detail.

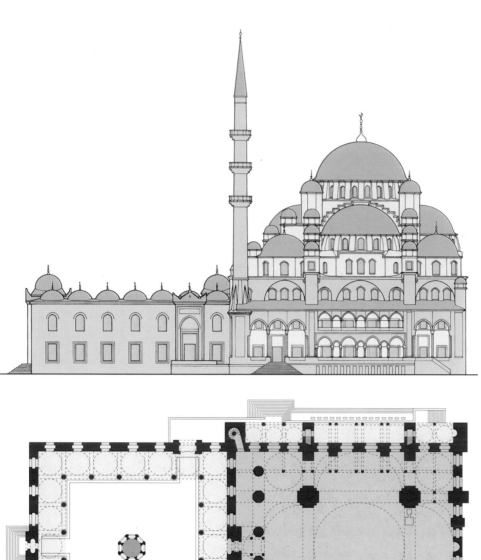

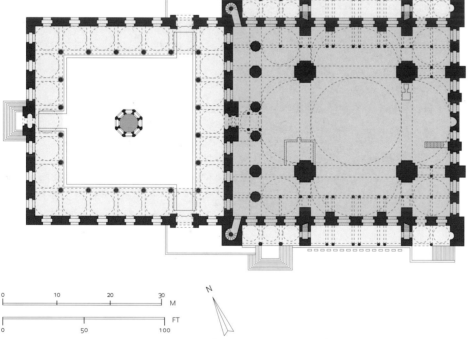

Homage to the Şehzade
Elevation and plan of the Yeni Valide Camii in Istanbul. Construction began in 1597 but was not finished until 1663; the architect was Sinan's pupil Da'ud Ağa. Its central plan, based on four semi-domes buttressing the central dome, reproduces that of Sinan's first masterpiece, the Şehzade. The language of Sinan is respected, and the verticality of the design confers a real elegance on this fine building.

the sole survivor of the disastrous Battle of Lepanto (1571) against the forces of Spain, Venice and the Papacy in which the Turks lost 228 galleys. The mosque forms the centre of a *külliye* comprising a *madrasa*, a türbe, a *hammam* and a public fountain.

The Kılıç Ali Paşa Camii is a beautifully executed replica, on roughly one-third scale, of Haghia Sophia. It is 38 m long, but, with the exception of its porch, it reproduces all the characteristics of its illustrious model: a central dome buttressed by two semi-domes, side-aisles formed by lateral galleries on two storeys, tympana resting on columns, and so on. Süleyman's ideas are here but expressed with diminished impact.

It seems impossible that the ninety-year-old Sinan should have returned to the Haghia Sophia model and designed such a project. It must surely be the work of his assistant, Da'ud Ağa, who had just completed the bazaar in the precinct of the Selimiye at Edirne. This imitation consequently belongs to the post-Sinanian era, just beginning, though Sinan continued to occupy the post of chief architect to the court until his death in 1588, and the Admiral's mosque therefore has a legitimate claim to his name.

After Sinan's death, Da'ud Ağa, an excellent practitioner but by no means so talented as his master, began to build and "sign" such works as the Yeni Valide Camii, opposite the Galata bridge in Istanbul. Begun in 1597, this mosque is in some respects a replica of the Şehzade, with its trefoil plan, four semi-domes around the central dome and square courtyard. It is the work of a worthy student of the master. But in the half-century since the Şehzade had been built, architecture had moved on, and Da'ud Ağa seems not to have noticed. The only indication that he had grasped the new developments comes in the apparent aspiration to a greater verticality, expressed in higher drums, hemispherical domes, and, in short, a vertical dynamic borrowed from Sinan's later work.

The Palace Complex: The Topkapı Sarayı

We have examined the superlative religious monuments commissioned by the sultans. Throughout the immense empire over which they ruled, they decreed the construction of charitable foundations, *külliye* established for the benefit of the poor and the ill, for pilgrim, warrior and dervish. But what were their own palaces like? What was the lifestyle of the sultans of the Sublime Porte?

Our image of the Ottoman palace is largely formed by the Topkapı Sarayı, which stands on the handsome promontory between the Golden Horn and the Bosphorus – on the very site where, two millennia previously, the temples of the Greek city of Byzantium had stood. The other palace buildings, such as those at Edirne, for example, have disappeared.

The Turks always felt a degree of nostalgia for the tent-villages of the nomad tribes. The incoherent, heteroclyte plan of the Topkapı Palace is proof enough of that. Over an area of nine hectares (roughly 450 by 200 m), the walled complex contains three separate zones. Behind the first gate, a huge space forms the first court; here were held official receptions, troop inspections, large-scale festivities and the exercises of the sultan's assembled guards. The court is closed to the south-east by utility buildings: kitchens, a bakery, and so on. According to Sinan's biographer, some of these buildings were designed by the master himself.

Opposite these buildings, to the north-west, are stone buildings fronted by porticoes. They include the Council Chamber, behind which the royal apartments and the Harem form a tangled mass of buildings, which seems to have been extended whenever extra space was required.

A gateway gives access to the third court. Immediately behind it stands the

A late Ottoman building
The elegant Library of the Topkapı Sarayı was built by Ahmet III in 1718. It has the finesse of classical Ottoman architecture.

The decoration of the palace
Detail of an İznik tilework panel of the kind for which the Topkapı Sarayı in Istanbul is famous. Carnations and garlands are delicately interwoven on the walls of the harem just as in the neighbouring mosques.

An elevated terrace
On the high terraces of the Topkapı Sarayı, the baldachin in bronze and gilded copper built by İbrahim I (1640–1648) presided over open-air receptions, which only friends and high-ranking guests of the sultan were allowed to attend.

Audience Chamber, a relatively small building presumably used for private audiences. Surrounded by a portico, it has been frequently restored, and contains the throne and baldachin. To the north, slightly off the central axis, is the library built under Ahmet III, in 1718, which exhibits clear signs of Western influence. The *hammam* on the right and a small mosque to the left depart from the orientation observed in the other buildings.

Behind a portico leading to the fourth court lies the most beautiful part of the palace. It contains, scattered among the lawns, a series of open kiosks, nestling amid trees or situated like belvederes where the view is best. They include the Bağdat Köşkü, from the reign of Murat IV, which was built to commemorate the capture of Baghdad in 1638; the Revan Köşkü, which commemorates the capture of Yerevan in 1635; and the *köşk* of Kara Mustafa Paşa, which dates from the mid-seventeenth century. The latter has two-storey rooms and its own small lake. The slender wooden structures of the kiosks, their low rooflines and the glass walls of their lower storeys give them a "modernist" aspect; indeed, they bring to mind the works of Frank Lloyd Wright. The kiosks do nothing to suggest the majesty and splendour of a sovereign.

This is an art of pleasure. Elegance replaces ceremony; light, open construction replaces monumentality; the effect is the antithesis of the pomp and solemnity of contemporary Western palaces. Even the *bergeries* (rustic cottages) of Marie-Antoinette at Versailles look a little solemn when compared with the Ottoman court. The kiosks' slight aura of impermanence harks back, perhaps, to the tents inhabited, centuries previously, by the nomadic chieftains of Siberia who became the sultans of Anatolia.

The belvedere of Murat IV
To commemorate the capture of Bağdat by Turkish forces in 1638, the Sultan Murat IV built the Bağdat Köşkü. This informal, asymmetrical construction is a fine example of Ottoman *joie de vivre*. The kiosk is set on a high base that raises it above the gardens, and its broad arcades are shaded by wide projecting eaves.

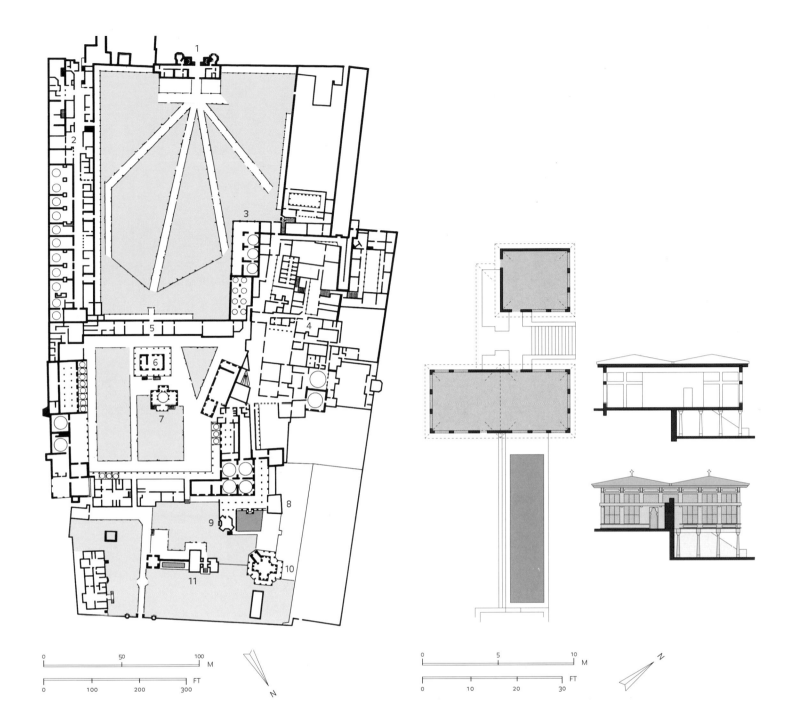

Plan of the Topkapı Sarayı

Various additions made by successive sultans have given the palace complex a rather disorderly appearance. **1** Orta Kapı (Middle Gate), **2** Kitchens and outhouses, **3** Guards' quarters, **4** Harem, **5** Bab-üs Saadet (Gate of Felicity), **6** Throne room, **7** Library of Ahmet III, **8** Circumcision Kiosk, **9** Revan Köşkü, **10** Bağdat Köşkü, **11** Sofa Köşkü.
Right: plan, section and elevation of the *köşk* of Kara Mustafa Paşa Sofa.

There is a striking contrast between these frame buildings, part of a palace whose infinite store of wealth was distributed through rooms of modest dimensions, and the magnificence of scale and ornament found in prayer-halls and other religious edifices. The Ottoman sultans displayed their wealth not in the palaces inhabited by the princes but in the construction and appointment of charitable and religious foundations.

The kiosks of Topkapı resemble nothing so much as the secondary residences of the wealthy denizens of Istanbul on the shores of the Bosphorus or the Sea of Marmara. There, the rich built pavilions and *yalis* – wood-frame houses whose living rooms nestle among trees or project out over the sea. Ruler and ruled alike showed a notable lack of ostentation. The great palaces, such as those of Dolmabahçe, were built later, in the eighteenth century, and were born of the fashion for things Western.

A "modern" kiosk
The south and east façades of the *köşk* of Kara Mustafa Paşa Sofa, also called Sofa Köşkü; it was built by the Grand Vizier of that name during the time he held office (1634–1663). The high proportion of glass in this very sober building gives it a modernist appearance surprising in an eighteenth-century construction.

Before its time
The north façade of the Sofa Köşkü exhibits a delicate construction and slender "pilotis" two hundred years earlier than the buildings by Le Corbusier and Frank Lloyd Wright that it brings to mind.

Wooden Town, Stone Mosques

Loggie
In the old Turkish quarters of Istanbul, traditional wooden houses of the kind inhabited by Ottoman city-dwellers still survive. The *loggie* overhanging the road are typical.

In most Turkish towns, Istanbul in particular, almost all housing, collective or individual, was built of wood. This was to said to lessen the impact of earthquakes. Towns tended to be extremely compact and irregular, with inextricable skeins of unpaved alleys and culs-de-sac winding through thickets of tall wooden houses. For the Istanbul of the Ottoman period, the great danger was fire. To avert catastrophe, watchtowers were built and watches appointed to signal any outbreak.

The town house differed little from the rural houses built in the forests. After all, most of Istanbul's inhabitants came from the provinces. Though the population of Constantinople was at a low ebb when it was captured – probably under 40 000 – there was an immediate influx of families from Anatolia and the Balkans. Early in Süleyman's reign, one hundred years after the fall of Constantinople, there were an estimated 400 000 people living in the capital, and this had, according to André Clot, risen to 700 000 by the early seventeenth century. Istanbul was by then the greatest city on the shores of the Mediterranean.

The population was crowded into three main quarters: Stamboul itself, the former Byzantium, on the promontory between the Sea of Marmara and the Golden Horn; Beyoğlu, on the European shore of the Bosphorus; and Üsküdar, on the Asian coast.

In the business districts, areas or streets would be given over to a particular trade, each under the wing of its trade guild; this was a medieval tradition common to East and West. Here leather workers congregated, here clothiers sold varieties of cloth. On one side of the street were the coppersmiths, on the other potters. One street was given over to spice-merchants, another to goldsmiths. Here were money-changers; food was elsewhere, and was itself divided into zones: in one butchers sold meat and live poultry in their stalls; in one street fruit was sold, in another fresh vegetables.

The diversity of products on sale was astonishing, as they came by sea and by land from every part of the Ottoman Empire. The port district was therefore among the busiest and most crowded of the city. The commercial harbour was entirely separate from the naval docks, which lay close to the arsenal and dominated the Tophane quarter.

Just as particular trades were located only in particular zones or streets, so the different communities – Arabs, Turks, Armenian Christians and Jews – for the most part lived separately. The sultans' policy towards the Jews was one of great tolerance, and they took in large numbers of those expelled from Spain. Another community was formed by Orthodox Greeks. The Catholic community, almost exclusively composed of merchants, was a small one, as the only Christian traders allowed to dock at Pera and Galata were the Venetians and Genoans who had opened trading posts.

To identify the communities of each zone, houses were painted a particular colour. This was not a symptom of discrimination. Ottoman society was tolerant, and non-Turks formed some forty per cent of the population of Istanbul.

After the swarming streets of the city, the Topkapı Sarayı, set in its gardens at the tip of a peninsula reaching out towards the Bosphorus, must have seemed an oasis of calm. The *külliye*, too, formed peaceful pockets, over which presided the domes of the great mosques: the Fatih Camii, the Süleymaniye, the Şehzade, and others. Their minarets gave Istanbul its characteristic skyline. From them, five times a day, the calls of the *muezzin* were heard, summoning the faithful to prayer.

The sombre wooden houses of the town, most of them with a tile revetment, must have formed a striking contrast with the pale stone and grey leaded domes of the mosques and *madrasas*. Nothing could make clearer the contrast between the ephemeral works of man and the "eternal" creations of religion.

AN IMMENSE EMPIRE

The Diffusion of the Ottoman Style

Despite military defeats such as the Battle of Lepanto (1571), and political reverses such as the liberation of the Habsburgs from tribute payment (1592), the Ottoman Empire survived largely intact until the end of the seventeenth century. Then the rout of the Ottoman troops beneath the walls of Vienna (1683) led to the formation of the Holy Alliance. In quick succession the Turks lost Hungary (1699), Dalmatia and the Morea (Peloponnese).

The first signs of decline manifested themselves at the death of Süleyman, in the person of his successor Selim II. And the defeat at Lepanto was a warning of things to come. Murat III seemed able to maintain the *status quo*; his generals defeated Persia. But the sanguinary Mehmet III (1595–1603), who ordered the execution of his son and nineteen brothers, had to ward off endless insurrections in Asia and put down a series of uprisings in Istanbul itself.

The Blue Mosque

Under Ahmet I (1603–1617), the Ottoman Empire lost Yerevan and Kars to the armies of Persia, and the sultan was forced to sign a highly disadvantageous peace treaty. During this reign the famous "Blue Mosque" or Sultan Ahmet Camii was built, between 1609 and 1617. It stands at the southern end of the Istanbul Hippodrome. It is, in part, a response to the nearby Haghia Sophia, and for visitors today it constitutes one of the most popular monuments of Turkish art. However, the mosque is far from innovative when compared to the late works of Sinan, and its most distinctive aspects are the wealth of polychrome decoration and the scale of the building.

The architect was Mehmet Ağa. He took his inspiration from the central plan adopted in the Şehzade, Sinan's first sultanic mosque, though the prayer-hall here is not square but rectangular. A notable feature of the building is the six minarets that rise above it. Their arrangement is unique, and eloquent of the influence of Sinan. Two of them are at the junction between hall and courtyard, as in the Şehzade; two stand at the front corners of the courtyard, echoing the layout of the Süleymaniye; and the final two are set on either side of the *qibla*, as if in imitation of the formula adopted by Sinan in the Selimiye.

The fact remains that the exterior of the Blue Mosque, and its position looking out over the Sea of Marmara, give it an undeniable splendour. Its courtyard is wider than it is deep and comprises nine domes by eight; the building as a whole measures 110 m long and 64 m wide, and the prayer-hall measures 52 m from entrance to *mihrab*.

There is a central dome some 23 m in diameter. It is buttressed by four semi-domes; there are smaller domes at the four corners. In architectonic terms, the mosque is a collection of quotations from the master. But this essay in Sinan's style is not a great success; the four piers from which the pendentives rise to the central dome are more than a little graceless. In this respect, the effect is rather of contrast than imitation.

The Blue Mosque
On the edge of the At Meydanı, or Hippodrome Square, the Sultan Ahmet Camii, with the Bosphorus beyond, raises its six minarets, which frame the prayer-hall and porticoed courtyard. The mosque, built between 1609 and 1617 by Mehmet Ağa, marks a return to the plan of Sinan's Şehzade and Da'ud Ağa's Yeni Valide Camii. To the right, in the foreground, the *madrasa* of the *külliye* of Sultan Ahmet.

The portico of the Blue Mosque
The proportions of the Sultan Ahmet Camii in Istanbul – it measures 110 m in length and 64 m in width – make it one of the great monuments of the Ottoman period. The two minarets flanking the entrance side of the courtyard possess only two galleries; the other four have three each.

The innovation here is the intensive use of tiles, to which the mosque owes its name. Tiles cover everything from the galleries upward, the only exception being stalactite work. And the many windows pierced in the walls and the drums of the dome and semi-domes are glazed with handsome polychrome glass. Size, spectacle, luxury, and brilliant colours are the main features of the Blue Mosque.

A monumental façade
The visitor entering the courtyard of the Sultan Ahmet Camii in Istanbul is greeted by the impressive façade of Mehmet Ağa's building. The rhythm of the portico and the increasingly large scale of the domes, all framed by the minarets, constitute a formidable architectural achievement.

The interior of the Blue Mosque
The Sultan Ahmet Camii in Istanbul owes its name "Blue Mosque" to the 20 000 or more ceramic tiles decorating the walls and arches of the prayer-hall. The mosque marks a return to the classic pattern of four semi-domes buttressing the principal, central dome. The latter rests on four enormous cylindrical piers of rather clumsy, squat form.

A utilitarian building
The Ottomans continued the work of the Selçuk Sultans in constructing caravanserais to provide staging-posts and to maintain strategic roads. In the heart of Anatolia, at İncesu in Cappadocia, this caravanserai was built in 1660–1680; it has a broad porticoed courtyard preceding the winter hall.

The portico at İncesu
The pointed arches of the arcades and the broad intersecting rib vaults notably lack the grace of Selçuk constructions.

Caravanserais and Palaces

The style of caravanserai built by the Selçuks in Anatolia some three hundred and fifty years before was by now outmoded, but the security of mail and trade crossing the country remained a matter of concern. Under Süleyman II, a fine Ottoman caravanserai was built at İncesu, in Cappadocia. Called the Kara Mustafa Paşa Hanı after the Grand Vizier, it was built in 1660–1680. The winter hall, situated behind a vast courtyard surrounded by vaulted porticoes, is roofed with intersecting rib vaults in finely dressed stone. The transversal bays are carried on a row of square pillars, from which rise pointed arches. Iron ties reinforce the structure. The large raised plinth along the walls, for traveller accomodation, is fitted with individual fireplaces for heating or cooking. The lower, central part of the hall was a stable.

The Deliller Hanı at Diyarbakır, not far from the city's Mardin Gate, also dates from the seventeenth century. Massive arcades on two levels precede the travellers' rooms. The black and white decoration of the walls makes play with alternating courses of stone and geometric motifs derived from stylised Arabic characters. Diyarbakır is not far from the Syrian border, and the Ottoman style has undergone local influences, manifest in both forms and craftsmanship.

Page 203
Powerful structures
The winter hall of the Ottoman caravanserai at İncesu is a veritable cathedral, with its sturdy pillars carrying arcades vaulted with intersecting and transverse ribs. Iron tie-rods link the square, unadorned pillars. Against the walls, the hooded fireplaces for individual use have their own chimneys.

Ablaq decoration
The alternation of dark and light stone (*ablaq* work) decorating the walls of the Deliller Hanı in Diyarbakır, built in basalt in the seventeenth century, reveals the influence of Ayyubid and Mamluk architecture.

A Syrian-Ottoman caravanserai
With its two levels of rooms set around the courtyard under vaults that exhibit further examples of *ablaq* decoration, the Deliller Hanı reflects the influence of neighbouring Syria. The restoration work has given new clarity to the remarkable ornamentation.

The effect of such stylistic "contamination" is still more obvious in a strange, indeed startling, building in the easternmost part of Turkey, not far from Mount Ararat (Turkish Ağri), on the site of Doğubayazıt. This is the Palace of İshak Paşa, completed around 1784. It was the princely residence of the Kurdish governors, who enjoyed semi-independence from the Ottoman state.

The most striking aspect of this complex, which stands in an eminently defensible position high in the mountains, is its syncretism. Behind an exemplary *pishtaq* in pure Selçuk style, with a stalactite niche, the courtyard façades offer superlative sculpted architraves in a style related to Armenian or Georgian work. Interlaced friezes, bands of animal motifs, and figures presenting four-way symmetry are immediately reminiscent of the Church of the Holy Cross (915) on Akhtamar island in Lake Van.

The mosque includes a prayer-hall, whose ceiling rests on slender columns supporting arcades and little domes. At the back, a dome set on squinches is lit by eight windows pierced in the drum. The cylindrical minaret with alternating red and black courses carries a stalactite gallery.

At the foot of Mount Ararat
Controlling a strategic pass between Turkey and Iran, the İshak Paşa Sarayı (palace), near Doğubayazıt, in the far east of Anatolia, was built by a Kurdish prince, and dates from the late eighteenth century. Within its double curtain walls rise the palace itself and a mosque and minaret.

Behind the mosque, the local ruler built apartments giving on to a courtyard probably once roofed. On either side, three arches resting on columns form a portico. Around the edge of the courtyard runs a plinth. The arcades are set on octagonal colonnettes and have slightly pointed arches, while the delicately sculpted capitals offer a great variety of motifs derived from *muqarnas*.

In short, the ornamental language of İshak Paşa Sarayı, realised in handsome pink stone, displays great imagination and combines a variety of traditions. It stands at the junction of many routes, and the discernible influences include Ottoman, Persian, Armenian, Georgian, Selçuk, and North Syrian art among others.

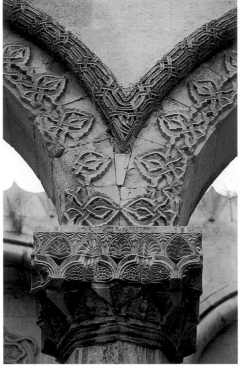

Ornamental detail
A stalactite capital in the Ottoman style is combined with garlanded voussoirs and a carved convex moulding in the palace of İshak Paşa, near Doğubayazıt.

A blend of influences
In the İşhak Paşa Sarayı the styles of Persia and eastern Anatolia converge. Behind one of the halls of the palace, which has lost its roof, rise the drum and dome of the mosque. The *ablaq* work in the minaret is further proof of the stylistic eclecticism of this complex.

Page 207
A collage of styles
The octagonal columns with their *muqarna* capitals, the slightly pointed arches, the blind semicircular arcades running along the walls, the rectangular frames of the windows, and the high plinth with geometric *ablaq* mosaic all form part of the extraordinary stylistic repertory of the İshak Paşa Sarayı. It was completed in about 1784.

Multiplicity of ornamental themes
Certain ornamental features appear in relief in the İshak Paşa Sarayı, near Doğubayazıt; they are reminiscent of Armenian ornamental techniques. The floral motifs, vine-leaves and grapes growing out of *canthari* derive from long-standing symbolic traditions.

Reminiscence and anachronism
In the late seventeenth century, the portal of the İshak Paşa Sarayı displays elements of the Selçuk idiom, with its stalactite niche under the arch of a *pishtaq* of Persian style; here the convex moulding is in stone, whereas in Persia it would be in brick.

A variety of arches

Beneath a dome supported by squinches, the prayer-hall of the mosque of the İshak Paşa Sarayı (like the palace itself) features both pointed and semicircular arches. It is thought that the *loge* of the princely ruler stood behind the five bays of the portico. The ruler of Doğubayazıt seems to have enjoyed a large measure of independence.

Hypostyle hall

A curious hypostyle hall stands next to the mosque itself in the İshak Paşa Sarayı. It has nine vaults and domes set on slender columns.

The seat of an Ottoman governor
The Azem Palace at Hamah in Syria was the seat of Asad el Azem, the illustrious *wali* of Hamah until 1749. Its raised terrace overlooks the river 'Asi (ancient Orontes). The style of this noble residence is a highly original synthesis of Ottoman, Ayyubid and Mamluk elements.

Wealth and distinction
The decoration of the portico leading into the reception room of the Azem Palace in Hamah combines mosaic flooring, alternating voussoirs and *ablaq* work, emphasising the prestigious nature of this half-private, half-public building.

Symbolic splendour

The *wali* received his guests under the dome, whose stalactite pendentives are illuminated by the oculus and the twenty lights let into the drum. The splendour of the room was destroyed during the revolt of Hamah in 1982; plans for restoration of the ruined shell are well advanced.

A profusion of ornament

The Azem Palace at Hamah dates from the first half of the eighteenth century and exhibits the luxury characteristic of the Islamic world: marble-veneered polychrome walls, gilded wooden furniture, a dome on stalactite pendentives, and a murmuring fountain between the three *iwans* of the reception room.

The Azem Palaces at Hamah and Damascus

Under the Ottoman Empire, the governors of distant provinces tended to behave like petty kings, a tendency that accelerated as the empire declined. This is illustrated by a fine example in Hamah, in Syria: the Azem Palace. It was, alas, badly damaged in 1982, when Israel clashed with Syria following the former's invasion of Lebanon. The palace takes its name from the governor Asad Paşa el Azem, the local *wali*. Its exterior has more or less survived, but the rather baroque attractions of the interior are known to us principally from pre-1982 photographs.

The merits of the building are not apparent to the casual visitor, for the house or *beit* (built in 1742) is hidden away in the labyrinthine old town of Hamah. Once you have found it, you must mount a narrow staircase to the first storey, before emerging on to a handsome terrace around which stands the porticoed façade of the building. From the apartments situated at the back of the palace there is a fine view of the banks of the river 'Asi (ancient Orontes).

The palace itself consists of a resplendent reception room in the form of an inverted "T". At the "crossing" there is a lantern dome resting on four large arches; the pendentives are covered in *muqarnas*. The rich polychrome marble, the gilded stalactite friezes, and the wooden ceiling whose honeycomb corners mask the transition between wall and ceiling, all testify to the *wali's* taste for luxury and elegance. These rooms formed a backdrop for the everyday life of a provincial potentate, and exemplify the transformation of Ottoman architecture under the influence of the Ayyubid and Mamluk buildings of Syria.

The stylistic convergence between Ottoman art and that of the Mamluks, who had been conquered in 1516 by Selim I, is a fine example of the victor assimilating the subject's style. The Azem Palace at Hamah – still more than that of Damascus, to which we shall return – demonstrates the longevity in Syria of the Mamluk style. The

The Azem Palace in Damascus
When the *wali* of Hamah was appointed Governor of Damascus in 1749· he took the title Asad Paşa el Azem, and built a new Azem Palace in Damascus, on a larger scale as befitted his new rank. The *haremlık* or private part of the house was constructed on a grand scale, which nevertheless retains a degree of intimacy.

Floral ornament

The delicate polychrome inlay ornamenting the joggled voussoirs of the Azem Palace in Damascus.

An attractive symmetry

The architecture of the Azem Palace (1749) shows considerable freedom in relation to Ottoman forms and techniques. Though the building is more overtly impressive than the kiosks of the Istanbul palace, it retains a certain simplicity.

Openwork in the spandrel
The porticoes of the Azem Palace
in Damascus (1749) display slender
columns and polychrome arcades.
In place of the Ottoman porphyry
discs, little scalloped circular bays
like oculi are let into the spandrels.

preference for polychrome marble rather than tile revetments, the stalactite friezes, the gilded wooden beams of the roof, and the capitals retain a stylistic continuity with those of the Sultans Qa'itbay or al-Ghuri of two centuries before.

The Azem Palace of Damascus, built in 1749 by the same Asad Paşa el Azem who had since become the Ottoman governor of Syria, is on a quite different scale. At its centre stands a huge courtyard, the *haremlık*, in the middle of which ponds and trees offer a welcoming shade and coolness. The buildings set around this open space are porticoed state rooms and a series of apartments with their own little *hammams*. The decorative style, as at Hamah, is very elaborate, making use of polychrome stone and wood. The relatively small rooms exhibit a degree of austerity, as in the palaces of Istanbul. Perhaps the most striking aspect of these Syrian residences is their lack of outward display. There is little or nothing externally to show that this is the dwelling of a governor.

Luxe, Calme et Volupté
Reflected in the pool which greets
the visitor at the entrance to the
Azem Palace in Damascus, the
portico creates a dream-like
atmosphere in this Turco-Arabic
residence of the mid-eighteenth
century.

A water maze
The fountains provide the musical
sound of water. In the Islamic
world, the purling of rivulets, the
murmur of fountains and the
mirror-surfaces of still water
define luxury.

A Lebanese palace
The summer residence of the
Emir Bashir II (a Druze who
governed Lebanon for the
Ottomans from 1810 to 1840),
the Beit ed-Din belongs in the
tradition of Damascene palaces.
Situated on the flank of a hill, it
is organised around a huge courtyard, whose two-storey portico
is of outstanding elegance.

A Lebanese Splendour

Further proof of the eclectic architecture of the Ottoman Near East is afforded by
the palace of Beit ed-Din, built in 1810 in the mountains of Lebanon for the Emir
Bashir II in a charming style.

As in the Azem Palace in Damascus, the Beit ed-Din is organised around a
handsome courtyard with a double portico on two storeys; its slender, airy arcades
are supported by octagonal colonnettes. A central fountain completes the vista.
There are also covered rooms or recesses, which are, like *iwans*, open on the façade
side; these seem to be Persian-style assembly rooms. The particular interest of the
palace is its position on the fringe of the Ottoman Empire, where local influences
predominate almost to the exclusion of the Ottoman character.

Right
The *diwan* of the Beit ed-Din
The reception hall features broad
divans on either side of a sort of
glazed veranda, in which the *emir*
would sit. The *diwan*, in Ottoman
tradition, is the seat of government: that is, of the sultan or his
representative.

A Turkish "baroque"
Western influence began to penetrate Ottoman style towards the end of the eighteenth century. The Nusretiye Camii in the Tophane quarter of Istanbul, built in 1823, exemplifies the neo-baroque style characteristic of the European effect on the Turkish arts.

Turkish "Baroque" in the Nusretiye Camii

In the provinces of the eastern Mediterranean, local influences progressively replaced the Ottoman aesthetic. In early-nineteenth-century Istanbul, it was Western influences which prevailed. The expanding European economies showed a dynamism that the Sublime Porte could no longer match, and exerted an irresistible attraction; this found expression in the architecture of Istanbul.

Perhaps the most characteristic example of the baroque style current in late Ottoman architecture is the Nusretiye Camii in the Tophane quarter. Here some of the ornamentation and the outline of the building as a whole suggest a "Louis XV style" which has its own eccentric charm. The combination of typically Ottoman structures, such as dome, minaret and tympana, with neo-baroque Western forms was the result of a compromise. The mosque was built from 1823 to 1826 under Mahmut II (1808–1839) by an architect named Kirkor Balyan, descended from an old family of Armenian builders.

A Western vocabulary
The structures of later Ottoman mosques present Western
baroque characteristics, but the
essential elements – the *mihrab*
and *minbar* – are retained in the
Nusretiye Camii in Istanbul.

Page 219
A domed prayer-hall
Despite its baroque ornament, the
Nusretiye Camii (1823) in Istanbul
continues the tradition of a large
dome supported by smooth pendentives and tympana. Late Ottoman buildings are little affected
by the baroque emphasis on
curved wall surfaces.

The mosque has no courtyard. Its square prayer-hall is dominated by the sultan's loge; a projecting chevet contains the mihrab. Twenty-four windows in the drum light the prayer-hall, whose dome rests on smooth pendentives set on four large arches.

This Westernised eclecticism had a precedent in works such as the Nuruos-maniye Camii, built between 1754 and 1757 near the Great Bazaar by Osman III (1754–1757). The plan of this mosque, with its semicircular porticoed courtyard, was something of a revolution within this conservative tradition. It was designed by an architect named Simon Kalfa, and presents a square prayer-hall capped by a single dome; the mihrab is in a semicircular apse.

The same kind of Turkish-Western syncretism is found in the Dolmabahçe Camii, also known as the mosque of Sultana Bezmialem, the mother of the Sultan Abdül Mecit (1839–1861); it was completed in 1853. Like the Nusretiye mosque, it com-prises a square prayer-hall with single dome and a minaret on either side. But the formal language of the building is entirely Western.

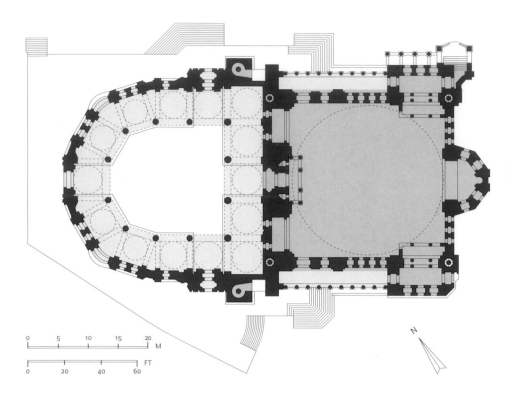

Ottoman Ceramics, Miniatures and Ornament

The most important single influence brought to bear on the aesthetic of the Selçuk
and Ottoman Turks was, self-evidently, that of Persia. This debt has been
mentioned in relation to certain architectural elements such as stalactite work and
*muqarna*s, which derive from the buildings of the Great Selçuks in Isfahan. We have
also spoken of the polychrome tiles made in Anatolia by Persian artists after the
Ottoman victory at Çaldiran in 1514. The capture of the Persian city of Tabriz that
year was a vital step in developing a Turkish ceramic industry, which was to be based
in İznik. Selim I forced 700 Persian ceramic-makers to emigrate to Anatolia with
their families; on arrival, they were ordered to impart their techniques. The products of these ceramicists adorned not only the mosques of Sokollu and Ahmet I at
Istanbul and the Selimiye at Edirne, but also the tables of the sultans, whose plates,
bottles and goblets were produced specially for the court.

With the art of ceramics came an ornamental repertory derived from the
fifteenth-century Timurid art of Persia. In Turkey, the vigorous and refined Timurid
aesthetic was adapted to Turkish tastes but retained many traces of its Persian
origins, notably floral motifs: carnations, roses, tulips, buttercups, with vine leaves
forming a luxuriant vegetation. In the sixteenth century, this influx of Persian
ornament, with its themes inspired by nature, quickly came to replace the geometric ornamental schemes of the earliest Ottoman art.

There was a further area in which the Timurid influence was felt: the art of the
book, and more particularly of the miniature. Indeed, after rather laborious begin-
nings during the Selçuk and early Ottoman periods, the emergence of a courtly art
of painting can be dated to the years after the capture of Tabriz. Several painters
and miniaturists of Persian origin came to the Istanbul court in 1515, and there they
formed a school, rather in the manner of the classical *scriptoria*.

But though the earliest Turkish illuminated books, from the mid-fifteenth
century, clearly exhibit the influence of Shiraz, they shortly afterwards underwent
a further influence, that of the masters of Herat. The Persian influence became still
more marked in the sixteenth century as the prestige of the court workshops of
Topkapı increased. The most beautiful manuscripts are those dating from the reign

The language of flowers
The Ottoman period produced a wide variety of decorative elements, some of them borrowed from Persia. İznik tiles are among the most perfect of these. This tiled panel with its chrysanthemum motif combines all the elements of the Ottoman floral repertoire.

The enchantment of flowers
Sixteenth-century Ottoman tiles present an inexhaustible wealth of plant motifs, and transform the mosque into a garden of Paradise.

of Süleyman the Magnificent and his direct successors down to Murat III. This was a blossoming of the illuminator's art, often of superlative quality, comparable to that of the Safavid era in Isfahan.

Among these works is the *Sulaymannama*, or *Book of Süleyman*, which forms part of the collection of the Topkapı Library. Completed in 1558, it covers the reign of the Sultan from 1520 to 1558. Though quite small – the format is 225 by 145 mm – its five volumes are a monument in themselves. The text was written by a chronicler named Matrakçı Nasuh, armour-bearer to the sultan. The miniatures were painted by several artists trained in the Persian schools, who worked alongside a Hungarian painter; the work of the latter was of particular assistance in the elegant portrayals of Western castles, towns and personages.

All the conventions of the Persian miniature are found in these superb illustrations. We recognise, for example, the several registers of unfolding perspective and the highly imaginative use of colour. The representation of architecture is highly individual and tends towards the fantastic. The text is written in Persian, by a calligrapher named Shirvani, whose name indicates his origins in northern Persia.

But there are other sources for the life of Süleyman, such as the Chronicle of Ahmed Feridun Paşa, which was given the honour of large-format illustrations: the pages are 300 by 200 mm. The work was dedicated to the Grand Vizier Sokollu Mehmet Paşa in 1568–1569.

The most original contribution to the Turkish art of the miniature is perhaps the *Siyar-i Nabi* or *Life of Mohammed*, six volumes made during the reign of Murat III, in the late sixteenth century. It is based on a text that was already two hundred years old, written during the second half of the fourteenth century, and follows the tale of a blind man called Darir from Erzurum, who told his story to the Cairo Mamluk Sultan Maliq Mansur. This vast illustrated biography of the Prophet was undertaken in the palace of Murat III; it required nothing less than the authority of an all-powerful sovereign to insist on the creation of a huge series of illuminations on the subject of the Prophet. For the prohibition on images in Islam is centred above all on Mohammed and the divine symbols. This series of 814 illustrations of the life of the Founder was therefore in breach of the most sacred rules.

Of the six volumes of the *Siyar-i Nabi*, Volumes I, II and VI belong to the Topkapı Library in Istanbul, Volume III to the National Library of New York, and Volume IV is in the Chester Beatty Library in Dublin. Volume V belonged to the Dresden Library and was lost, presumably destroyed, during World War II.

Another famous manuscript dating from the reign of Murat III is particularly worthy of attention. It is the *Hünername*. This very large work (490 by 310 mm), of which only the first two volumes survive, deals with the history of the Ottomans, and is illustrated by the famous master Osman. The paintings are, without exception, of the very highest quality. The text is the work of Sayid Loqman, historiographer to the sultan, and this chronicle is perhaps the greatest single work of art devoted to Turkish history.

The Persian influence persists throughout the history of the Ottoman miniature, but the style of representation becomes increasingly individual. Whereas the Timurid or Safavid conventions imposed an aristocratic perspective, Turkish miniatures often present a freer, more spontaneous and even humorous vision of things.

Turkish painting of the eighteenth century tended, like Turkish architecture, to undergo a Western influence that eventually sapped its originality. But in this sudden flowering of the art of the miniature, as in the floral motifs of tile revetments, the arabesque designs of carpets, and generally in the minor decorative arts of the Ottoman period, we perceive the underlying influence of a Persian aesthetic. And this conclusion is all the more surprising if we consider that architecture itself had been – with the exception of themes such as stalactite work, open-work panels and ornamentation in general – almost entirely purged of Persian influence.

Page 222 above

The *Life of Süleyman*

Among the most famous manuscripts of the Topkapı Sarayı is the *Sulaymannama* (*Book of Süleyman*), the five volumes of which were completed in 1558. It records, in exhaustive detail, the receptions, campaigns and successes of the sultan. The miniaturist's art, partly derived from the Timurid style, gives us an insight into the protocol of the court in the mid-sixteenth century. (Library of the Topkapı Sarayı Museum, Istanbul)

Page 222 below

The image of the Prophet

In defiance of the Islamic prohibition, the cycle of the *Siyar-i Nabi* depicts significant moments in the life of the Prophet. The cycle comprises six volumes and was completed during the reign of Murat III. In this miniature, the body of Mohammed is enveloped in golden flames and his face is hidden by a mask. His wife, Fatima, is also represented. (Library of the Topkapı Sarayı Museum, Istanbul)

Left

Music and dance at the court

The *Sulaymannama* (1558) depicts a feast given by the sultan: musicians and dancers organise a reception amid the luxuriant decoration. The conventions of representation derive from Timurid miniatures. (Library of the Topkapı Sarayı Museum, Istanbul)

Right

Süleyman at war

This scene from the *Sulaymannama* shows the sultan in his camp during the siege of a Christian fortress in Hungary. Süleyman, in his state tent, conveys his orders to his troops, while the helmeted defenders of the castle await the assault. (Library of the Topkapı Sarayı Museum, Istanbul)

CONCLUSION

The Originality of Turkish Architecture

Selçuk ornament

Characteristic of the proliferating ornament of the Rum Selçuk Sultanate, this detail from the Sultanhanı, near Aksaray (1229), combines tracery, stalactites and friezes with the zig-zag fluting of a "salomonic" column; the capital is carved with stylised acanthus leaves.

It is important to draw the conclusions implicit in this summary overview of 600 years of Selçuk and Ottoman architecture, in relation both to the other currents of Islamic architecture and to the legacy of the great buildings of humanity.

At the time of the Rum Selçuks, the current of Islamic architecture was driven by building techniques founded on quarrystone, and focused on vaulted spaces rather than the traditional Arab hypostyle prayer-hall. The influence of the Romano-Byzantine world was decisive in this respect. A further important influence was the continental climate of Anatolia: torrid summers and cold, sometimes snowy, winters. These were the preconditions. The result was building on an increasingly large scale: mosques, *madrasas* and caravanserais. The winter halls of the caravanserais testify to the role played by Armenian and Syrian masters in the public works of the Selçuk sultans; they constituted a link with antiquity, allowing medieval Anatolian architecture to develop along the lines indicated by Romano-Byzantine technology.

But the adoption of pointed arches and a geometrical style of ornament led, on the one hand, to increasing rigour of and design, on the other to a blossoming of architectural ornament. The crumbling of authority under the Turkoman Emirates in the late thirteenth century transformed this architectural language. With the emergence of the Osmanlı tribe as a ruling power came closer contact with the Byzantine heritage. This, and the transformation of Orthodox churches into mosques, led to the creation of longitudinal spaces in place of the transverse rectangle of Islamic religious tradition. A new type of mosque made its appearance: it generally had a single dome as well as internal spaces comprising two halls placed one behind the other. This describes the religious buildings of Bursa. But even before the fall of Constantinople this type of mosque had been replaced by another. The prayer-hall was now a single, square room capped with a hemispherical dome. From this point on, that majestic and formidable ancestor, the church of Haghia Sophia, haunted the architectural forms of the Ottoman world. Both Hayrettin and Sinan drew on it for inspiration, though the model it so imperiously offered was transformed in their hands.

The resplendent architectural successes of the reigns of Bayezit II and Süleyman I testify to the alternating attraction to and revulsion from the Byzantine model experienced by the Turkish architects of the sixteenth century. But this period was also that of the Renaissance in the West, and though the nations of the Holy League were ranged against it, the Ottoman Empire was not immune to Western influence. However antagonistic the two cultures competing for the lands of classical civilisation, there were points of contact. There were ambassadors and merchants. Genoa and Venice both had trading posts in the Ottoman Empire, and the Ottomans sought to create links with Italian artists by inviting them to the Seraglio. They also commissioned the master smiths of the Holy Roman Empire to come to Istanbul and create the artillery they needed.

Treaties were drawn up, notably with François I of France. People travelled, and ideas travelled with them. Fruitful contacts were made. One result of this was the

Imperial splendour
Detail of the decoration above the sultan's *loge* in the Süleymaniye (begun 1550). The most powerful sovereign of the Ottoman period reduced the emblematic decoration in his Istanbul mosque to bare essentials.

striking similarities perceptible between Eastern and Western buildings sometimes of identical date. We may cite the courtyard arcades of the Bayezit II mosque in Edirne and those of Brunelleschi's Spedale degli Innocenti in Florence; or the central plans adopted by Sinan and that of Santa Maria della Consolazione in Todi, sometimes attributed to Bramante. Of course, the relative stability of the Ottoman dynasty allowed for a greater continuity in architectural enterprises. With few exceptions, a single architect designed, then oversaw the construction of a mosque and its *külliye*. By contrast, in Italy major undertakings such as the new St Peter's basilica in Rome were subject to quarrels, interruptions, changes of architect, and financial crises which brought construction to a standstill. The unity of the design tended to suffer.

What is most striking about Ottoman architecture of the sixteenth century is precisely the profound coherence of the buildings. From the ground up, rules and forms are imposed with a vigour, logic and unity that command our admiration. Ideas are carried to their logical conclusions; the rigour of these constructions challenges comparison with the finest buildings of the West. Perhaps Michelangelo and Palladio alone are equal to the comparison. It is this quality of self-evident rightness that constitutes the perfection of Sinan's architectural language; it led him to an ever greater austerity of form. The priority that he accorded volume and space – sometimes at the expense of ornament – gave his works a luminous simplicity. They became a hymn to the logic of geometrical beauty, a spatial harmony in which rhythm is made stone. Proportions and measurements combine in a timeless revelation of the monolithic certainties of the immanent.

Page 227
A symbol of Ottoman architecture
A cascade of domes on the Sultan Ahmet Camii in Istanbul exemplifies the development of one of the chief glories of Ottoman architecture.

CHRONOLOGICAL TABLE

Ankara, *mihrab* of the Arslanhane Camii

Diyarbakır, Ulu Camii. Detail of the façade

Monuments

8th century	Mardin: Ulu Camii, original Arab building
	Diyarbakır: Ulu Camii, original Arab building
after 1091	Diyarbakır: transformation of Ulu Camii
1100	Sivas: Ulu Camii

1155	Silvan: Ulu Camii
1156	Konya: Alaeddin Camii begun, completed in 1220
1192	Tercan: Mama Hatun Kümbet
1217	Sivas: Şifaiye Medresesi
1218	Hekimhanı caravanserai

622–1100	**1100–1220**
Turkish Invasions	The Crusader Invasions

Historical Events

622	Hegira: the beginning of Islam
663	Islam spreads to Asia Minor
751	Arab defeat of China at Talas
962	Ghaznevid Sultanate founded
962	Nicephorus Phocas recaptures Aleppo for Byzantium
1038–1063	Tügrül Beg rules as Ghaznevid sultan
1051	Tügrül Beg conquers Persia
1055	Tügrül Beg captures Baghdad
1063–1073	Alp Arslan Turkish sultan
1071	Selçuks defeat the Byzantines at Manzikert
1073–1092	Melik Şah sultan
1081	Rum Sultanate Süleyman Prince of Nicaea (modern İznik)
1097	Konya (Iconium) Rum Selçuk capital
1099	Crusaders capture Jerusalem

1107–1116	Melik Şah sultan
1116–1155	Masud I sultan
1155–1192	Kılıç Arslan II sultan
1176	Selçuk defeat of Byzantium at Myriocephalon
1190	Crusaders besiege Konya
1192–1196	Keyhüsrev I sultan. He unifies Anatolia
1204	Crusaders capture Constantinople and establish Latin Empire in Byzantium
1204–1210	Second reign of Keyhüsrev I Mongol invasion
1219–1236	Keykubad I at Beyşehir

Niğde, Alaeddin Camii

Konya, dome of the Büyük Karatay Medresesi

Sadeddin Han, portico

Erzurum, arcades of the Çifte
Minare Medrese

1221 Konya: city walls
1223 Niğde: Alaeddin Camii
c. 1224 Kayseri: citadel
1229 Sultanhanı near Aksaray
1230 Antalya: Yivli Minare
1232 Sultanhanı near Kayseri
1235–1236 Sadeddin Han
1236–1246 Kırkgöz Hanı
1237 Kayseri: Huant Hatun Camii
1242 Ağzı Kara Hanı (near Aksaray)
1246–1249 Konya: Horozlu Han

1253 Erzurum: Çifte Minare Medresesi
1255 Konya: Büyük Karatay Medresesi
1265 Konya: İnce Minare Medresesi
1271 Sivas: Gök Medrese, Çifte Minare
Medresesi, Muzaffer Bürüciye
Medresesi
1275 Kayseri: Döner Kümbet
1296 Beyşehir: Eşrefoğlu Camii

1308 Erzurum: Yakutiye Medresesi
1312 Niğde: *türbe* of Hudavent Hatun
1338 Kayseri: Köşk Medrese

1220–1250
Selçuk Empire

1250–1300
The Artistic Apogee

1300–1350
The Rise of the Ottomans

1221–1237 Keykubad I sultan
1237–1246 Keyhüsrev II sultan
Mongol invasion
1243 Keyhüsrev defeated by the
Mongols at the Kösedağ: the
Sultanate a protectorate

c. 1250 A Mongol representative governs
alongside a Turkish sultan
Late 13th Turkoman Emirates
century
1284–1308 Keykubad II, last Selçuk sultan
1298–1324 Osman I in Bithynia

1326 End of the reign of Osman, who
founds the Ottoman dynasty. Prusa
(Bursa) is captured and becomes the
Ottoman capital
1326–1359 Reign of Orhan Gazi who organises
the Ottoman armies
1331 Capture of Nicaea (modern İznik)
1346 John VI Cantacuzene gives his
daughter in marriage to Orhan

Hall of the Sarıhan
near Avanos

Beyşehir, interior of the
Eşrefoğlu Camii

Kayseri, basalt wall of
the citadel

Edirne, hospital of the *külliye*
of Bayezit II

1484–1488	Edirne: *külliye* of Bayezit II by Hayrettin
1489–1588	Life of the architect (*mimar*) Sinan of Kayseri
1501–1506	Istanbul: Bayezit Camii by Hayrettin
1520	Istanbul: Selimiye, completed in 1522
1543–1548	Istanbul: sultanic mosque called Şehzade
1547	Istanbul: preparations for the building of the Süleymaniye

1358	Gevaş: *türbe* of Halime Hatun	1421	Bursa: Yeşil Türbe		
1366	Manisa: Ulu Camii	1426	Bursa: Muradiye		
1378	İznik: Yeşil Camii	1437–1447	Edirne: Üç Şerefeli Camii		
1391–1400	Bursa: Yıldırım Bayezit Camii	1451	Bursa: *türbe* of Murat II		
1396	Bursa: Ulu Camii	1452	Istanbul: Rumeli Hisari		
1419	Bursa: Yeşil Camii	1463–1471	Istanbul: first Fatih Camii and *külliye*		

1350–1420
The Early Ottoman Period

1420–1470
Capture of Constantinople

1470–1550
The Power of the Ottomans

1360–1389	Murat I sultan
1361	Ottoman capture of Adrianople
1365	Adrianople, renamed Edirne, becomes the Ottoman capital
1389–1403	Yıldırım Bayezit I sultan. First siege of Byzantium
1393	Ottoman conquest of Bulgars
1402	Tamerlane defeats Bayezit. Civil war between Bayezit's sons
1405	Death of Tamerlane
1403–1413	Interregnum
1413–1421	Mehmet I sultan

1421–1444	Murat II sultan for first time
1422	Constantinople besieged
1444–1446	Mehmet II sultan for first time
1446–1451	Murat II sultan for second time
1448	Conquest of Serbia
1451–1481	Mehmet II Fatih (the Conqueror)
1453	Capture of Constantinople. Constantinople becomes Istanbul

1481–1512	Bayezit II sultan
1485–1491	Bayezit II defeated by the Cairene Mamluks
1512–1520	Selim I sultan
1514	Selim attacks Shah Ismail Capture of the Upper Euphrates
1517	Conquest of Mamluk Empire: Turkish sultans become Caliphs
1520–1566	Süleyman the Magnificent sultan
1521	Capture of Belgrade
1529	Siege of Vienna fails
1534	Capture of Tabriz and Baghdad
1540	Peace concluded with Venice and the Empire

Manisa, interior of the Ulu Camii

Bursa, Yeşil Camii, sultan's *loge*

Istanbul, interior of
the Süleymaniye

Istanbul, Library of
the Topkapı Sarayı

1550–1557 Istanbul: Süleymaniye
1553 Damascus: Tekke of Süleyman
1556 Istanbul: Haseki Hürrem Hamamı
1558 Istanbul: Mihrimah Camii,
completed in 1565
1563 Uzunkemer aqueduct
1566 Istanbul: Süleyman's *türbe*
1570 Istanbul: Sokollu Mehmet Paşa
Camii
1567–1574 Edirne: Selimiye Camii
1577 Istanbul: Azapkapı Camii

1580 Edirne: bazaar of the *külliye* by
Da'ud Ağa
1582 Istanbul: Kılıç Ali Paşa Camii
1597 Istanbul: Yeni Valide Camii by Da'ud
Ağa begun
1609–1617 Istanbul: Sultan Ahmet Camii
(Blue Mosque)

1635 Topkapı: Revan Köşkü
1638 Topkapı: Bağdat Köşkü
1680 İncesu (Cappadocia): Kara Mustafa
Paşa Hanı
1718 Topkapı: Library of Ahmet III
1742 Hamah: Azem Palace
1748 Istanbul: Nuruosmaniye Camii
1749 Damascus: Azem Palace
1784 Doğubayazıt: Ishak Paşa Sarayı
1810–1840 Lebanon: Beit ed-Din palace
1823 Istanbul: Nusretiye Camii
1853 Istanbul: Dolmabahçe Camii

1550–1580
The Artistic Apogee

1580–1620
Gradual Decline in Architecture

1620–1860
The Close of the Ottoman Era

1556 Ottoman defeat at siege of Malta
1565 Mehmet Paşa Sokollu Grand Vizier
1566 Death of Süleyman
1566–1574 Selim II sultan
1571 Disaster at the Battle of Lepanto
against Spain, Venice and the
Papacy; the Turkish fleet
is destroyed

1574–1595 Murat III sultan
1592 Habsburgs freed from tribute obligation
1595–1603 Mehmet III sultan
1603–1617 Ahmet I sultan

1656 The Köprülü dynasty of viziers hold
power until 1710
1669 Capture of Crete
1699 The Sublime Porte is expelled from
Hungary, Dalmatia and the
Peloponnese
1736 The Sublime Porte under attack
from Russia and Austria
1757–1774 Mustafa III sultan
1768–1774 War against Russia
1774–1789 Abdül Hamit I sultan
1789–1807 Selim III sultan

Edirne, dome of the Selimiye

Istanbul, the Blue Mosque

GLOSSARY

Abbasids: the second dynasty of → Caliphs, which succeeded the → Omayyad Caliphate of Damascus in 750. Its authority began to wane in the late tenth century, but was not finally extinguished until the Mongols put the last Abbasid Caliph to death in 1258.

Ablaq: decorative system based on alternating black-and-white or dark-and-light layers of stones or arch-stones.

Abraham: venerated in the Torah and the Bible as the Jewish patriarch, he is considered the ancestor of the Jewish and Arab peoples through his sons Isaac and Ismael. For Muslims, he is "God's friend", and is supposed to have founded the → Kaaba in Mecca.

Arcade: architectural element composed of arches resting on a series of pillars, piers or columns. An arcade can form a → portico.

Ayyubids: independent Islamic dynasty, founded by the Kurd Salah ed-Din, better known as Saladin. It reigned from 1171 to 1260 over Syria, Upper Mesopotamia, Egypt, the Yemen, and the holy cities of Mecca and Medina.

Bagratids: a native dynasty, which reigned over Armenia from 885 to 1079.

Basileus (plural basileis): Greek royal or imperial title assumed by the Byzantine sovereigns from 650 on.

Bay: transversal spatial unit in a roofed space, the space between two columns. The bay is in contrast to the → nave, which is the longitudinal spatial unit.

Beit: Arabic for "house".

Caliph: head of the Islamic community in line of succession from the Prophet. The Caliph is the "Commander of the Faithful". The Turkish sultans acquired the title of Caliph during the reign of Selim I, who conquered Mamluk Egypt in 1517.

Cami (Camii): Turkish word deriving from Arabic term *jami* meaning "that which assembles" and referring to congregational mosques.

Caravanserai: in Muslim countries, a fortified staging post on trade or pilgrimage routes. The Selçuk and Ottoman caravanserais marked the staging posts of camel caravans, which travelled some 25 to 30 km daily.

Circumambulation: a religious practice: walking around a holy place as a sign of veneration and piety. In Islam, the practice is particularly associated with the → Kaaba at Mecca, and the mausolea in which the powerful or the holy were buried.

Cyma recta: a classical moulding comprising a double curve, of which the upper part is concave and the lower convex.

Danishmendites: Turkish tribe, which formed its own Emirate in north-west Anatolia. It governed from the late eleventh century to 1178, and was overthrown by the Sultan Kılıç Arslan II.

Depressed arch: → Four-centred arch.

Dervishes: mendicant or other Islamic monks subject to a mystic rule.

Dikka: raised stage in a mosque, from which the officiant directs the prayers.

Divan: Persian term for the sovereign's council.

Emir: Arabic title designating a military commander, later a governor of a province.

Four-centred arch: a pointed arch shaped so that the joints of the → voussoirs converge on four points, forming the radii of four circles. The shape resembles the upturned hull of a boat; the corresponding vault is sometimes called a keel vault.

Ghazi: Arabic term describing the Muslim combating the infidel. In Turkey, a title bestowed on the victorious warrior.

Ghaznevids: Turkish dynasty, which reigned over Afghanistan and the Punjab in the tenth and eleventh centuries.

Hammam (Turkish hamamı): public or private baths following the Roman model, with cold, warm and hot rooms. The speciality of Turkish baths is a very hot steam room.

Han: → *khan* and caravanserai.

Haram: the consecrated area of the mosque, in which prayer is said and rituals take place. Usually the prayer-hall; may include the whole sacred area.

Hegira: literally the "expatriation" of Mohammed, when he left Mecca for Yathrib, which became Medina, the City of the Prophet (Medinat al-Nabi). This event took place in 622, and marks the beginning of the Islamic era.

Hypostyle hall: a hall whose roof is supported by rows of columns or pillars forming many aisles and bays.

Imam: Arabic term meaning the leader in ritual prayer (literally: "he who stands in front"). For the Shiites, the *imam* is the head of the religious community, the heir to the Islamic tradition, and the interpreter of the teachings of the Prophet.

Imaret: refectory or soup-kitchen for the poor. *Imarets* are often found as part of a → *külliye*.

Intrados: the lower or interior curve of an arch or → voussoir.

Iwan: vaulted architectural space in the form of a large niche. It usually opens on to a courtyard; it is surrounded by a flat frame. The form is of Persian origin.

Jihad: Arab term for "holy war" waged against the infidel.

Kaaba: sacred centre of Islam in Mecca where the Black Stone is venerated in the sanctuary founded by → Abraham, according to tradition. It is the object of the pilgrimage or *haj* instituted by the Koran, which every practising Muslim must carry out at least once in his life.

Karamanid: Turkoman dynasty in Anatolia, established in the thirteenth century in the Konya region. It was conquered by the Ottomans.

Keystone: stone, usually wedge-shaped, at the summit of an arch.

Khan (or han): a caravanserai, or, in towns, a warehouse in which merchants could deposit their goods in safety.

Khanqah: Arabic name for an Islamic monastery. The monks

were usually mendicants but could be soldiers.

Kiosk: from the Turkish *köşk*, designating a pleasure pavillion open on all sides and built in light materials such as wood.

Koran: literally "recitation": the sacred book of Islam, which contains the teachings of the Prophet Mohammed.

Külliye: Turkish term for the complex of buildings belonging to a charitable foundation set around a mosque. It normally comprises one or more → *madrasas*, a hospital-dispensary, a → *khanqah* (monastery), an asylum for the insane, a fountain for ablutions (→ *şadırvan*) and → *türbes* (tombs).

Kümbet: synonym for → *türbe*.

Lantern tower: a little tower, pierced with windows, which crowns a dome or roof, and allows light to flow into the interior.

Limes: Latin for "boundary", used for the fortified borders of the Roman Empire.

Loggia: an open gallery or arcade; the box from which the sultan watched rituals.

Madrasa: → Sunni Koranic school. Often built in the form of a traditional Persian courtyard mosque with → *iwans*. The Turks built many *madrasas* in their attempt to restore regions influenced by → Shiite doctrine to Sunni Islam.

Mamluks: soldier-slaves, often of Turkish origin, who took power in Egypt and India and formed powerful dynasties.

Mihrab: niche capped by a semi-circular vault and preceded by an arch set in the → *qibla* wall. It indicates the direction of Mecca, toward which Muslims turn to pray.

Minaret: high tower from the top of which the → *muezzin* five times a day issues the call to prayer.

Minbar (mimber, minber): raised pulpit to the right of the → *mihrab* from which the preacher addresses the congregation in a mosque.

Muezzin: chants the call to Islamic prayer from the top of the minaret. The words he sings out are: "Allah is greater. I witness that there is no other God than Allah. I witness that Mohammed is the emissary of God. Come to Prayer. Come to Salvation". The first *muezzin* is said to be Bilal.

Muqarna: stalactite ornamenting the corbels of a building. These honeycomb vaults gradually ceased to have any structural function.

Nave: longitudinal main space running along the central section of a temple, mosque or church.

Oculus: round opening in the summit of a dome.

Omayyad: Islamic Arabic dynasty said to have descended from the Prophet which succeeded the first → Caliphs, those of Medina. Established in Damascus, it was founded by Mu'awiya in 660 and came to an end in 750 in the Near East. In Moorish Spain, where it ruled from 756, it survived until 1031.

Osmanlı: member of the Ottoman dynasty. The Osmanlıs are the Ottoman tribe.

Ottomans: dynasty of Turkish sultans, founded in the thirteenth century by Osman I. It reigned over a vast empire, and came to an end only in 1922, having attained the apogee of its power in the sixteenth and seventeenth centuries.

Pendentive: architectural term designating the concave spherical triangles forming the connection between a square plan and the circular base or drum of a dome. To be distinguished from the → squinch.

Peribolus: (Greek) consecrated area enclosing a temple.

Pishtaq: Persian term designating a portal with a wide frame and a niche in the form of an → iwan. Found as the gateway to mosques, → madrasas, → khanqahs, and → caravanserais.

Portico: structure composed of weight-bearing elements – pillars or columns – which support a façade or the interior of a covered space. The portico can have either architraves or arches; if the latter, it is called an → arcade.

Qibla (kible): the wall of the mosque that stands at right angles to a line between the mosque and Mecca. It contains a niche called the → *mihrab*. In prayer, Muslims bow down toward the *qibla*.

Rum (Selçuks): Rum refers to the *Rumi*, or Romans, here meaning the Byzantines. The Rum Selçuk Empire (1073–1308) included Anatolia and expanded on to the north bank of the Bosphorus and into western Europe.

Şadırvan, sebil: fountain in the courtyard of a mosque used for ritual ablutions. Water was distributed free for those requesting it.

Safavids: → Shiite dynasty, which reigned over Persia between 1502 and 1736. Under Shah Tahmasp I, it ceded Mesopotamia to the Ottoman sultans. But Shah Abbas I the Great restored the Persian Empire.

Samanids: Iranian Islamic dynasty, which reigned in Persia and Transoxiana between 874 and 999. It included Khorasan and Seistan; its capital was Bokhara.

Sassanids: Persian dynasty and principal rival of Romano-Byzantines. It reigned from 224 to 651 over an empire that extended from Mesopotamia to the Indus. It was destroyed by the lightning advance of the Arab tribes in the mid-seventh century.

Scotia: concave moulding between two → *tori* in base of classical pillar.

Scriptorium (plural scriptoria): space in a monastery set aside for copying manuscripts.

Selamlık: male quarters of Ottoman residence or palace.

Selçuks: this dynasty of sultans of Turkish Central Asian origin reigned over Iran and Iraq in the eleventh and twelfth centuries. The Selçuks captured Baghdad in 1055 and defeated the Byzantines at Manzikert in 1071, progressively occupying Anatolia. Thereafter the Great Selçuks of Iran are distinguished from the → Rum Selçuks of Asia Minor.

Seraglio: a sultan's palace.

Shiites: a sect of Islam devoted to the tradition represented by Ali, the husband of the Prophet's daughter, Fatima, whom they consider to have inherited the Caliphate by direct line.

Spandrel: triangular space between the side of an arch and its rectilinear frame; also applied to the surface between two arches in an → arcade, and the surface of a vault between adjacent ribs. This area is often decorated, especially around the → *mihrab*.

Spolia: (Latin: "spoils, plunder") reused elements from classical buildings.

Squinch: small diagonal vault set on a diagonal and vaulting a re-entrant angle. The four squinches that carry a dome transform a square opening into an octagon. They thus allow the circular base of a dome to be carried on a square opening.

Stalactites: → *muqarna*.

Stereotomy: the art of cutting the stone of which a building is made.

Sunni: the Islamic orthodoxy, founded on the *Sunna*, the law constituted by the Koran and the *hadiths* (conversations of the Prophet), which together form the Islamic traditions. The Sunni believe that men appoint the → *imam*, as opposed to the Shiites, who hold that God does.

Tekke (tekkiye): Turkish equivalent of → *khanqah*.

Temenos: Greek for "a piece of land sacred to a god", in particular a temple precinct.

Torus (plural tori): convex moulding on base of classical columns.

Tunnel vault: vault of semicircular profile.

Türbe: Turkish term for a mausoleum. This was generally a round, octagonal or other polygonal building containing a funerary chamber and capped by a high conical roof.

Turkish pleats: architectural formula original to the first Ottoman architects, in particular at Bursa. It constitutes a geometric transition between square plan and dome, and is composed of projecting triangular folds. It performed the functions generally fulfilled by → pendentives and → squinches.

Turkish triangle: a form of connection between the square plan of a building and the circular base or drum of the dome. It forms a rectilinear (not concave) triangular surface at the four corners of the building, and replaces the → pendentive and → squinch.

Tympanum: vertical surface between a door lintel and a surmounting arch; the wall area filling in an arch or pediment.

Voussoirs: wedge-shaped stones forming the structure of an arch on either side of the keystone.

Wali: Ottoman regional governor.

Yali: Turkish secondary residence, built in wood at the edge of the sea, whose reception room may project out over the shore.

Bibliography

Akurgal, Ekrem: *L'Art en Turquie,* Fribourg, 1981.

Aslanapa, Oktay: *Turkish Art and Architecture,* London, 1971.

Atil, Esin: *The Age of Sultan Süleiman the Magnificent,* New York, 1987.

Babinger, Franz: *Mahomet II le Conquérant et son temps (1432–1481),* Paris, 1954.

Barkan, Ömer Lufti: "L'organisation du travail dans le chantier d'une grande mosquée à Istanbul au XVIᵉ siècle", in: *Annales, Économies, Sociétés, Civilisations,* 6, 1962.

Braudel, Fernand: *La Méditerranée et le monde méditerranéen à l'époque de Philippe II,* Paris, 1949.

Creswell, K. A. C.: *Early Muslim Architecture,* 2 vols., Oxford, 1932, 1940.

Cuneo, Paolo et alii: "L'architecture", in: *Arts de Cappadoce,* Genève, 1971.

Dagron, Gilbert: *Constantinople imaginaire,* Paris, 1984.

Egli, Ernst: *Sinan, der Baumeister osmanischer Glanzzeit,* Zürich, 1954.

Encyclopédie de l'Islam, 1st edition, Leyden, 1913-1938, 2nd edition, Leyden, 1960, in progress.

Erdmann, Kurt: *Die anatolische Karavansaray des 13. Jahrhunderts,* 3 vols., Berlin, 1961–1976.

Gabriel, Albert: "Les Mosquées de Constantinople", in: *Syria* VII (1926), pp. 359–419.

Gabriel, Albert: *Les Monuments turcs d'Anatolie,* 2 vols., Paris, 1931–1934.

Goodwin, Godfrey: *A History of Ottoman Architecture,* Baltimore, 1971.

Gurlitt, Cornelius: *Die Baukunst Konstantinopels,* 2 vols., Berlin, 1912.

Hoag, John D.: *Western Islamic Architecture,* New York, 1963.

Inalcik, Halil: *The Ottoman Empire, Conquest, Organization and Economy,* London, 1978.

Kühnel, Ernst: *Islamic Art and Architecture,* London, 1966.

Mantran, Robert: *Histoire de la Turquie,* Paris, 1952.

Michell, George (ed.): *Architecture of the Islamic World,* London, 1978.

Roux, J.-P.: *Histoire des Turcs,* Paris, 1984.

Scheja, Georg: "Hagia Sofia und Templum Salomonis", in: *Istanbuler Mitteilungen,* 12, Tübingen, 1962.

Soliman le Magnifique et son temps, Rencontres de l'École du Louvre, Paris, 1992.

Stchoukine, Ivan: *La Peinture turque d'après les miniatures illustrées,* Paris, 1966.

Stierlin, Henri: *Architecture de l'Islam, de l'Atlantique au Gange,* Fribourg, 1979.

Stierlin, Henri: *Architecture islamique,* Paris, 1993 (= Que sais-je).

Stierlin, Henri: *Islam de Bagdad au Cordue, Des origines au XIIIᵉ siècle* (= Taschen's World Architecture), Cologne, 1996.

Stierlin, Henri: *Soliman et l'Architecture ottomane,* Fribourg, 1985.

Stratton, Arthur: *Sinan,* New York, 1972.

Tanindi, Zeren: *Siyer-i Nebi,* Istanbul, 1984.

Ünsal, Behçet: *Turkish Islamic Architecture in Seljuk and Ottoman Times,* London, 1973.

Vogt-Göknil, Ulya: *Turquie ottomane,* (= Architecture universelle, 14), Fribourg, 1965.

Yerasimos, Stéphane: *La Fondation de Constantinople et de Sainte-Sophie dans les traditions turques,* Paris, 1990.

Yerasimos, Stéphane: Istanbul, *La mosquée de Soliman,* Paris 1997.

Yetkin, Suut Kemal: *L'Architecture turque en Turquie,* Paris, 1962.

Index – Monuments

Index – Persons

Acknowledgements and Credits

The publisher, author and photographers of this work on the architecture of Selçuk and Ottoman Turkey would like to thank the Turkish authorities for the facilities they made available at sites and museums while it was being researched. We should particularly like to thank the Ministry of Culture at Ankara, the Directors and staff of the Museum and Library of the Topkapı Sarayı in Istanbul, and the Tourist Board of the Kayseri region.

Photographic acknowledgements:

Page 3: © The Metropolitan Museum of Art, New York

Pages 13, 200–201 and 205: © Giovanni Ricci, Milan

Page 34: © Roland and Sabrina Michaud / Rapho, Paris

Pages 38, 199 and 227: © Werner Neumeister, Munich

Page 74, middle left: © Francescini – Zodiaque, Saint-Léger Vauban

Page 74 bottom left: © Dieuzaide – Zodiaque, Saint-Léger Vauban

Page 75 left: © Zodiaque, Saint-Léger Vauban

Page 198: © Maximilien Bruggman, Yverdon

We would particularly like to thank Alberto Berengo Gardin for the plans on pages 9, 25, 27, 28, 29, 35, 46, 51, 72, 73, 80–81, 83, 85, 92, 96, 101, 104, 110, 117, 119, 120, 126, 127, 130, 143, 146, 153, 157, 162, 171, 172, 182, 184, 189 and 220.

ALL 40 TITLES AT A GLANCE

Each book: US$ 29.99 | £ 16.99 | CDN$ 39.95

"... a truly remarkable publishing event in architecture."
The Architectural Review
London

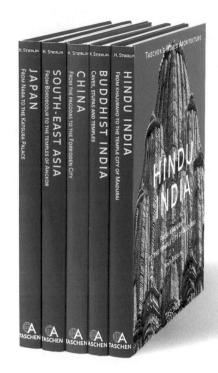

▶ Collect 40 volumes of TASCHEN'S WORLD ARCHITECTURE in eight years (1996—2003) and build up a complete panorama of world architecture from the earliest buildings of Mesopotamia to the latest contemporary projects.

▶ The series is grouped into five-volume units, each devoted to the architectural development of a major civilisation, and introducing the reader to many new and unfamiliar worlds.

▶ Each volume covers a complex architectural era and is written so vividly that most readers will feel the urge to go out and discover these magnificent buildings for themselves.

TASCHEN'S WORLD ARCHITECTURE

"An excellently produced, informative guide to the history of architecture. Accessible to everyone."
Architektur Aktuell, Vienna

"This is by far the most comprehensive review of recent years."
Frankfurter Rundschau, Frankfurt

"A successful debut of a very promising series."
Architektur & Wohnen, Hamburg, on *Islam from Baghdad to Cordoba*

"...each theme is presented in a very interesting, lively style... it makes you want to set off straight away to see everything with your own eyes."
Baumeister, Munich, on *The Roman Empire*

▶ TASCHEN'S WORLD ARCHITECTURE presents 6000 years of architectural history in 40 volumes.

▶ Each volume is a detailed and authoritative study of one specific era.

▶ The whole series provides a comprehensive survey of architecture from antiquity to the present day. Five volumes will be published each year.

▶ TASCHEN'S WORLD ARCHITECTURE is a must for all lovers of architecture and travel.

▶ Renowned photographers have travelled the world for this series, presenting more than 12000 photographs of famous and lesser-known buildings.

▶ Expert authors guide the reader through TASCHEN'S WORLD ARCHITECTURE with exciting, scientifically well-founded texts that place architecture within the cultural, political and social context of each era.

▶ The elegant, modern design and the clear, visually striking layout guide the reader through the historical and contemporary world of architecture.

▶ Influential architectural theories, typical stylistic features and specific construction techniques are separately explained on eye-catching pages.

▶ Each volume includes between 40 and 50 maps, plans and structural drawings based on the latest scholarly findings and are produced for this series using state-of-the-art computer technology.

▶ The appendix contains clear chronological tables, giving an instant overview of the correlation between the historical events and architecture of any given civilisation.

▶ A detailed glossary clearly explains architectural terms.

▶ An index of names and places ensures quick and easy reference to specific buildings and people.

▶ Each book contains 240 pages with some 300 color illustrations on high-quality art paper. 240 x 300 mm, hardcover with dust jacket.

Each book: US$ 29.99 | £ 16.99 | CDN$ 39.95